CW00646780

Pelagius
INQUIRIES AND REAPPRAISALS

BY THE AUTHOR

Studies in Pelagius

FOUR LETTERS OF PELAGIUS
PELAGIUS: INQUIRIES AND REAPPRAISALS

Pelagius
INQUIRIES AND REAPPRAISALS

———◆◈◆———

ROBERT F. EVANS

WIPF & STOCK · Eugene, Oregon

Wipf and Stock Publishers
199 W 8th Ave, Suite 3
Eugene, OR 97401

Pelagius
Inquiries and Reappraisals
By Evans, Robert F.
Copyright©1968 by Evans, Robert F.
ISBN 13: 978-1-60899-497-7
Publication date 3/17/2010
Previously published by Seabury Press, 1968

To Lilian

Preface

————◆————

ONE can scarcely read and certainly not write a book about Pelagius without being aware of the problem, raised acutely by Georges de Plinval, of the British monk's extant literary remains. I have given attention to that problem in *Four Letters of Pelagius* (New York: The Seabury Press, 1968). In the chapters which follow, I have assumed conclusions reached in that study, viz., that of Plinval's claims for Pelagius there is at present evidence for assigning to him only the following letters: *De vita Christiana, De virginitate, Ad Celantiam,* and *De divina lege.*

In the year 1965–66 I was the fortunate recipient from the Hazen Foundation of a Lilly Post-Doctoral Fellowship in Religion. To that foundation and to the University of Pennsylvania, I am grateful for a year of uninterrupted research and writing in the preparation of this book. To the most cordial and cooperative staff of the University Library at Tübingen, I am thankful for superb working facilities and for a large number of services. In typing the manuscript and in inserting many revisions, Mrs. Hilda H. Rifkin gave generously of her time, patience, and humor.

R.F.E.

University of Pennsylvania
May, 1967

ix

Contents

Abbreviations Used

Works of Pelagius:

Cel.	*Epistola ad Celantiam* (CSEL 56, 329–56)
De lege	*De divina lege* (PL 30, 105–16)
De lib. arb.	*De libero arbitrio*, fragments in Augustine, *De gratia Christi* and *De peccato originali* (CSEL 42, 123–206); additional fragments edited by Alexander Souter in PL Supplementum 1 (Paris, 1959), 1539–43.
De nat.	*De natura*, fragments in Augustine, *De natura et gratia* (CSEL 60, 231–99)
Dem.	*Epistola ad Demetriadem* (PL 30, 15–45)
Ep. ad Innoc.	*Epistola ad Innocentium*, fragments in Augustine, *De gratia Christi* 32–45 and *De peccato originali* 19–22 (CSEL 42, 149–59 and 179–82)
Exp.	*Expositiones XIII epistolarum Pauli*, ed. Alexander Souter (Texts and Studies IX, 3 vols., Cambridge, 1922–31)
Lib. eclog.	*Liber eclogarum* (called by Augustine also *Liber capitulorum* and *Liber testimoniorum*), fragments scattered through Jerome, *Dialogus adversus Pelagianos* (PL 23, 518–60) and Augustine, *De gestis Pelagii* (PL 44, 319–60); these fragments collected by Garnier, PL 48, 594 f.
Lib. fid.	*Libellus fidei* (PL 45, 1716–18)
Trin.	*De fide trinitatis*, fragments in PL Supplementum 1 (Paris, 1959), 1544–48, 1549–57
Virg.	*De virginitate* (CSEL 1, 224–50)
Vita	*De vita Christiana* (PL 40, 1031–46)

Pelagius

INQUIRIES AND REAPPRAISALS

Chapter 1

---◆◆◆---

INTRODUCTION

PELAGIUS and the heresy called by his name continue to provide occasion for careless slogans and confident postures. In centers of theological learning, the cry "Pelagianism" is inevitably hurled whenever the schemes of men appear to threaten the necessity and sufficiency of the divine grace. The author of a recent and provocative book on Christian ethics seeks to clarify his conception of the divine promise of human fulfillment offered in the gospel by contrasting his own position with "Pelagianism" on the one hand and "fideism" on the other. As over against the former, he announces the thesis: "The primal implementation of the promise is the human deed done by God in the Cross: human deed, because Jesus Christ is a man who acts for his fellow men; done by God, because God was in Christ reconciling the world to himself." [1] Pelagius would unquestionably have agreed and would have been puzzled by the association of his name with the contrary of such a thesis.

But Pelagius would have been equally puzzled over the approbation accorded to his name by some of his self-styled modern friends. A humanist psychiatrist whose books are widely read in America calls Pelagius to his side as he delineates the features of "humanistic" religion and contrasts this with the "authoritarian" religion represented by Augustine and the Catholic Church.[2] But since the chief virtue in "authoritarian" religion is obedience and its cardinal sin

1

·disobedience,[3] the frequent and emphatic appearance of these moralistic concepts in Pelagius does not encourage us to find in him a simple antithesis to "authoritarian religion." Nor does Augustine's rich doctrine of healing grace, flowing from the fount of being in the Godhead, restoring a structure of order and peace to a human nature otherwise torn by inner disorder and strife—nor does this doctrine quite fit the psychiatrist's polemical formula, "authoritarian religion."

I make these observations only by way of applying to our present subject the commonplace that those who concern themselves with the history of ideas must pick their way carefully through a dense growth of misleading slogans. This is not to claim that the general categories under which the history of Christian doctrine is usually presented are entirely wide of the mark. It is of course true that Pelagius was condemned as a heretic for teaching an insufficient and erroneous doctrine of grace, for teaching also a correlative doctrine of the possibilities of human achievement which appeared to deny the necessity of grace. It is true also that Pelagius' understanding of the term "grace" is a very deficient one when regarded from the point of view of Augustinian theology. But it is not the case that the issue between Pelagius and his opponents can be formulated by the simple questions: Are grace and the divine initiative necessary for salvation? Are men apart from the gospel bound by the power of sin? The questions are, rather: What is the nature of that grace that is necessary for salvation? What is the nature of that solidarity in sin by which men are bound? And beneath these more immediate questions lies a more fundamental one: What is the nature of man, who is bound in sin and in need of the divine grace?

But so to state the questions leading to the heart of the controversy over Pelagius is already to jump over some interesting matters with which the earlier essays in this book will be concerned. The reader of a book on Pelagius might perhaps expect to find some treatment of the details of his life so far as they are known, an account of his theological teaching, a delineation of the contrasting theology of St.

Augustine, and a description of the events of controversy which led to final condemnation. Treatments of this general sort are easily available, and the reader is encouraged to consult them for the filling up of lacunae left by the present volume.[4] The chapters that follow are presented in the belief that the present state of scholarship justifies a more piecemeal and exploratory approach than would be the case if another more general book on Pelagius were now to be offered. There are questions concerning the career and writings of Pelagius which continue to hang suspended over the total picture, questions which deserve consideration in detail. To an exploration of some of these, the first four of the following essays are devoted.

Whenever we hear the name of Pelagius, we are conditioned by long schooling immediately to summon up the name of Augustine and to consider the important historical and theological issues to center on the antithesis of these two figures. I do not mean to suggest that this fundamental evaluation should be abandoned. It was, after all, Augustine who led the African agitation which was successful in securing both the imperial banishment and the final papal condemnation. And it was Augustine supremely whose theological position against the Pelagians was to commend itself to both Catholic and Protestant orthodoxy, although the former never completely assimilated the whole of Augustine's theology in its final form. But to say this much is to admit that the common and all but involuntary habit of jumping to a comparison of Pelagius' theology with the anti-Pelagian theology of Augustine is conditioned to a high degree by particular theological and ecclesiastical considerations. The respective interests of the theologian and of the historian are not necessarily antithetical, but they do not necessarily coincide. In the case of the matter at hand, a closer attention to some of the relevant historical data will, on the one hand, enlarge our knowledge and understanding of Pelagius himself and, on the other hand, qualify our appreciation of the theological antithesis between him and Augustine.

If we adopt a chronological approach to Pelagius as a controversial figure, we find him in the Holy Land and in conflict with Jerome well over a year before Augustine made him a specific target of attack in 415. The animosity between Jerome and Pelagius concerns a nice nest of issues which will be examined in Chapters 2 through 4. The writings of Jerome have in regard to Pelagius been relatively unexploited, yet they offer interesting clues and throw significant light upon the man. To approach Pelagius through Jerome makes a great deal of sense, as I hope will become clear in these chapters. Jerome knew Pelagius by personal acquaintance in Rome during the 380's, whereas Augustine knew him only through his writings. Jerome was already at odds with Pelagius as early as 394, almost two decades before "the Pelagian controversy" began. In spite of his hostile tendentiousness, Jerome was able to formulate Pelagius' theological position with quite reasonable fairness in the writing of his anti-Pelagian dialogue. He had sufficient knowledge of his opponent's theological background and practice as a teacher to be able to point us toward a most important source book for Pelagius' theology, the enchiridion of Sextus, a comparison of which with the writings of Pelagius will be offered in Chapter 4.

Not the least aspect of Jerome's importance for the study of Pelagius is the fact that the latter's two polemical treatises *De natura* and *De libero arbitrio* were written within the context of the conflict with Jerome and express their author's reaction to that doctor's teaching on the character of sin as a necessary aspect of human corporeal existence. When the first of these came under Augustine's scrutiny in 415, at that moment and not until that moment the Bishop of Hippo decided that Pelagius was a highly dangerous character, so dangerous in fact that nothing but imperial banishment and papal condemnation would do. The date of Augustine's open declaration of war is of interest in that he had already known of Pelagius' important teachings for some three years. Chapter 5 will examine the significance attaching to Augustine's entrance into the battle specifically against Pelagius in 415.

What is here offered then is a series of discrete yet inter-related essays on Pelagius and the early phases of the Pelagian controversy, a series which begins with evidence offered and suggested by Jerome, then moves to a consideration of Augustine's relation to Pelagius, and concludes with an attempt at a balanced exposition of Pelagius' theology.[5]

Chapter 2

---◈---

PELAGIUS AND THE REVIVAL
OF THE ORIGENIST
CONTROVERSY

Studies in recent decades have not paid sufficient attention
to Jerome in measuring the significance and activity of Pelagius. This has no doubt been the case in part because Jerome
is tendentious and at points quite untrustworthy. Surely the
critic is not to be taken seriously who wants to make us
laugh with the picture of a huge dolt, grown wide and thick
from Scottish porridge, plodding along at the pace of a
turtle.[1] At a more theological level, one has looked askance
at Jerome's way of seeing in the teaching of Pelagius a rep-
resentation of heresies which he detested, particularly those
of Jovinian and Origen.[2] In this as in other matters, a skep-
tical approach to Jerome is the only proper one. On the other
hand, Henry Chadwick has with justice remarked as follows:
"But perhaps it is the secret of Jerome's great skill as a
master of the indelicate art of invective that while much of
his torrential abuse is wild, exaggerated, and extremist, there
is almost always some grain of truth in the charge; it is es-
sential to the effectiveness of his attack that while it is un-
reasonable it is never wholly deficient in truth—or at least
in verisimilitude." [3] In this and later chapters of this book,
we shall see that such a judgment upon Jerome's view of
Pelagius is far from inaccurate.

6

It may not be out of place to venture another reason why Jerome has not been fully exploited: Pelagius has tended to possess significance for scholars as the opposite pole to Augustine. Even if one is prepared to admit that Augustine himself gives only a partial view of his opponent, which needs correction in the light of Pelagius' own writings, the tendency has been nonetheless present to direct investigation toward a final important question, viz.: What is the relation of Pelagius' thought to prevailing Western conceptions of grace and of the relation of grace to works? That this is an interesting and important question need not for a moment be denied. But preoccupation with this underlying question has tended to produce, I suggest, something like the following implicit judgments: because Jerome had neither a very clear nor an interesting doctrine of grace with which to oppose Pelagius, he therefore was deficient in his understanding of the real issue, and his continual raising of the ghosts of Jovinian, Origen, and Rufinus betrays only the mentality of a haunted and battle-scarred old man. These judgments are, at least from a historian's point of view, unwarranted.

When Jerome at Bethlehem began to write his commentary on Jeremiah in about the year 414,[4] he was an aging and indeed an anxious man. Jeremiah alone among the prophets he had not yet made the subject of a commentary, and he was determined to get on with it.[5] Yet from the beginning he was clearly distracted by troubling issues which the arrival of Pelagius in the Holy Land had raised. Before beginning to write on Jeremiah he had taken time from his exegetical work to write the letter[6] to Ctesiphon against Pelagian teachings. At some point after composing the preface to the fourth book of the commentary, Jerome very likely laid the work down for a time and wrote his dialogue against the Pelagians,[7] which we know to have been in progress in July, 415.[8] The commentary, then, is written in distraction and in the midst of composing polemical works against the Pelagians. Jerome's concern is evident at many points in the commentary itself. In every one of the prefaces to the individual books except that to the sixth and last are to be found unmistakable references to Pelagius and his disciples, and in the body of the commentary Jerome takes occasion no fewer than twenty-two times[9] to attack one or more points of Pelagian teaching. Ulysses in the Sicilian straits stopping his ears against the lethal songs of the Sirens—that is the image by which Jerome points to his own distraught effort to move on with the commentary and to ignore the lies being spread about by the devil. The devil himself is mute, Jerome goes on to inform us, and is doing his present barking through the big fat Alpine dog, a dog who in this case is able to rage more effectively with his heavy heels than with his teeth.[10]

We understand this rhetoric properly if we see that Jerome is, on the one hand, displaying his deep uneasiness and, on the other, affecting scorn that Pelagius has no bite. Jerome is uneasy not simply because Pelagius has arrived in the vicinity, teaching certain doctrines about free will and the possibility of sinlessness. One may doubt that *Jerome* would have allowed himself to become so unsettled if that were all that was at stake. Rather, his profound sense of disturbance arises from the fact that Pelagius has come upon the scene reviving past charges against Jerome, charges which the old fighter had every reason to hope were long buried. But the dog's teeth are really not terrifying because in reviving the old charges Pelagius is in part using arguments not at all original with him but which he has got from others, preeminent among whom was Rufinus of Aquileia. In his fondness for canine imagery, Jerome, making this same point, can identify Pelagius and his friends with the mute dogs of Isa. 56:10, seized with the mad will to lie, but deficient themselves in the art of composing lies.[11]

The revived charges against Jerome were of two sorts: (1) that in his commentary on Ephesians, Jerome had used passages and ideas from Origen in a very surprising way for one who was to declare his attitude to Origen as always having been antiseptically free of heresy;[12] (2) that in his treatise against Jovinian, Jerome had gone too far in his depreciation of marriage.[13] The revival of these two charges was certain to be upsetting, because they touched two of the weakest points in Jerome's long history of controversy. The supposition that Jerome could have been imagining Pelagius' revival of these charges has nothing to commend it. In no sense would it have been to his interest to have these matters again brought to anyone's attention. Indeed, he specifically remarks that such charges as are now being made on the matter of Origen have already been disposed of;[14] his new critics are regrettably unaware that in his letter[15] to Pammachius he once and for all cleared up whatever ambiguities there might have been in his books against Jovinian, and such arguments as Pelagius is now advancing are but the ravings of men long since buried.[16] It might also be observed that Pelagius' actual revival of the charges would have lent plausibility to Jerome's repeated assertions[17] that Pelagius is a disciple of Jovinian, of Origen, and of Rufinus.

In this chapter I shall consider the significance of the first of these charges, saving the second for the next chapter.

The matter of Jerome's use of Origen in his commentary on Ephesians had first been raised by Rufinus in his *Apology* some thirteen years before. The intention of Rufinus had been to argue that Jerome had turned his back upon the master from whom he had learned so much, and to point out that in his commentary on Ephesians, written *ca.* 387–389, he had in fact accepted opinions of Origen which he was later to disown, opinions on such matters as the resurrection, the pre-existence of souls, and the restoration of the devil.[18] In selecting the commentary on Ephesians for attention, Rufinus was simply accepting a challenge which Jerome himself had laid down. In a letter to his Roman friends Pammachius and Oceanus, Jerome had carelessly invited his critics to inform themselves of his consistently held opinions by reading his work on Ephesians. There they would find that he had always opposed the doctrines of Origen.[19] The implication underlying Rufinus' examination of passages in Jerome's commentary is that judging by his opinions in 401, Jerome was once a heretic and ought now to disown what he once wrote.[20] And is the absurdity not patent of branding as a heretic a man whom one has once hailed as the teacher of the churches second only to the Apostles? [21] Rufinus writes, of course, as the translator and warm advocate of Origen, firmly believing the master's works to have been interpolated at points where unorthodox teachings are to be discerned.[22]

In his three-volume *Apology* against Rufinus, Jerome attempts *inter alia* to deal with the probings of his adversary into the commentary on Ephesians.[23] Rufinus, says Jerome, does not understand the first rudimentary principles governing the writing of commentaries. Jerome had simply followed the long-standing practice of both sacred and secular commentators in introducing the opinions of authors other than himself with a view to allowing the reader to choose the most satisfactory interpretation.[24] The author is to be held responsible only for what is left when the opinions of other commentators whom he has used have been extracted.[25] Both in the commentary on Ephesians and in other exegetical works, he had given interpretations of others as well as his own, "while openly declaring which views are heretical and which are catholic." [26] At the very most, his fault was that of not identifying the authors whom he was employing.[27] And besides, no reader of the commentary on Ephesians has any right to be scandalized by finding offensive opinions there, since Jerome had forewarned the reader in the preface that he would find views of other writers there, especially Origen, Apollinaris, and Didymus.[28]

The dispassionate reader of Rufinus and Jerome is brought inevitably to the conclusion that on this matter Rufinus has a legitimate point, which his opponent is rigidly determined not to concede. The position of the modern reader is complicated by the fact that Jerome did not wait to receive the full text of Rufinus' *Apology* before composing the first two books of his own work and instead relied upon written reports from friends at Rome.[29] It is in the first book that Jerome deals at length with points concerning the commentary, only briefly mentioning the matter in the third book, when he has Rufinus' text in front of him.[30] It is even less surprising, therefore, than it would have been otherwise that at places Jerome misses the point that Rufinus is making.[31] Nor does the fault lie all on one side. Rufinus occasionally presses a small detail too hard and makes Jerome responsible for an implication that is at best far fetched.[32] But when every allowance has been made, the judgment is inescapable that Jerome is fighting recklessly with his back to the wall, unwilling to admit that he was once tolerant of opinions now despised.[33]

There is manifest inconsistency between two of Jerome's contentions in the *Apology* as to his approach to Origen in the commentary. It can scarcely be true both that he has simply included opinions and arguments of Origen in order that the *prudens lector* might decide upon them for himself, and that he has consistently warned the reader which interpretations are heretical and which catholic.[34]

We may take up Jerome's challenge to compare his commentary on Ephesians with another of his exegetical works. Let us select the one that he himself suggests[35] as showing equally well his constant opposition to the doctrines of Origen: the commentary on Ecclesiastes, written in 388–389.[36] Here Origen makes three easily identified appearances, two of which it will be instructive to examine. The third is less interesting for our purpose, concerning a noncontroversial interpretation of Eccles. 4:13–16. One might note, however, that in this third case the views of Origen and Victorinus, which are said not to differ greatly, are summarized together and set down after fairly long quotations from Gregory Thaumaturgus and Apollinaris, which Jerome in turn has placed after his own comments.

In explaining the thought of the Preacher at 1:9 f. that that which has come to pass is that which will come to pass and that nothing under the sun is new, Jerome first says that the text "seems" to be speaking in a general way about such phenomena as the process of procreation, human birth and death, the rising and setting of the sun, the relation of the land masses to the sea, the flying of birds, and the swimming of fish.[37] Then, having noticed the similarity in thought between the verses under consideration and a sentence from Terence, he goes on to quote some lines which he says he has read *in quodam libro*. The quoted words interpret the verses from Ecclesiastes as referring to the creation of man in an age previous to this one: "Man had an existence, therefore, before he was made under the sun." [38] Jerome appears at first to reject such a line of interpretation with the observation that we would have to suppose other things as well to have been created before this world—draft horses, plants, and all manner of small and large animals. But he then goes on himself to explain that the interpretation in question will hold up if one adopts the view that it is only man who is here said not to be new under the sun. One may argue this plausibly on the basis of verse 10: it is precisely that being who could say of himself, "See, this is new," who has had an existence in previous ages; since animals cannot speak or say such a thing, not to mention plants, it is man alone whose existence "under the sun" is not new.[39] Most interestingly Jerome now goes on himself to observe that this interpretation of verse 9 as it is related to verse 10 is consistent with his own interpretation of verse 9. That is, one can suppose that nothing new happens within this world in the general sense that Jerome had outlined, while holding also to the view that man's existence "under the sun" is not a new one, since man's existence antedates the sun.[40] Jerome is here far from warning against the Origenist doctrine of man's premundane creation.

Later Jerome comments on the pessimistic thought, in verses 2 and 3 of chapter 4, that he who has not been born or seen the evil that is done under the sun is better off than both the dead and the living. Here he first gives his opinion that the text means it is better not to exist at all than either to know the evils of this world while still living or to pass beyond them in death, naked as from a shipwreck. In particular, the text does not mean, he thinks, that the yet unborn are happier because they have not yet been weighed down by bodies. He then goes on to state in greater detail the Origenist exegesis, with its theory of the descent of souls into bodies, while prefixing to this account the following introductory words: "But others understand this passage as follows." [41] Here, we may say, is a case of Jerome's having carried out something like what he was later to claim had been his consistent practice. He states his own view, he states the Origenist view, and he registers his disagreement with the latter.

In view, however, of Jerome's position as stated in the *Apology*, we must say the obvious—that in the commentary on Ecclesiastes his practice falls short of his later claims. In the first case above, he puts forward in support of the Origenist view an argument with which at the very least he appears not to disagree, and expressly writes that the interpretation in question is consistent with his own. In neither case above is it yet a question of his own "catholic" view opposing a "heretical" view. Yet in both cases the Origenist teaching in question is that of the premundane existence of souls, a doctrine included specifically among the eight propositions which Jerome was later to join in censoring. [42]

The work on Ecclesiastes may give us a point of comparison and a perspective upon the question of the use of Origen in the commentary on Ephesians. It is evident that Jerome in 401 and in 417 did not have an entirely inaccurate memory about his employment of Origen in the exegetical works of 387–389. As we have seen, he did in fact juxtapose the opinions of other commentators beside his own, now with no evaluative comment at all, [43] now signifying his disagreement with greater or less emphasis. [44] He could register his disagreement with Origen's doctrine of the premundane souls, but he could also acquiesce in it. In fact the shrillness and recklessness of the later polemic is no doubt due to the fact that Jerome was well able to remember part of the truth but did not want to remember all of it. [45]

Not long after laying down his work on Ecclesiastes, Jerome began and finished the commentary on Ephesians with breathtaking haste.[46] About a third of the way to the end he admits that on some days he dictates a thousand lines.[47] With this haste goes a notable carelessness in the manner of inserting material from Origen. But besides any mere carelessness Jerome is obviously at points clearly drawn to Origenist views. We find that in his work on Ephesians Jerome is much less careful than in the commentary on Ecclesiastes to draw any line between an independent interpretation of his own and one which he takes from Origen.

It is quite true that Jerome does warn the reader at the end of the prologue to the work that he will draw upon material from Origen as well as from Apollinaris and Didymus. But there is no hint that this warning is in the interest of preparing the reader to distinguish acceptable from unacceptable views. Rather, in informing the reader that he has "in part followed" Origen and that "this work is partly that of others and partly my own," Jerome seems much more to be serving notice of a sort which in a later day would fall under the rubric of "academic honesty." [48]

In the body of the commentary we may first notice Jerome admitting that at 2:12 he is drawn to the notion of a premundane creation of souls with its accompanying theory of the acquisition of varying degrees of merit before the descent into bodies, in order adequately to explain why St. Paul is able to say that "we have hoped *beforehand* in Christ." [49]

When he comes to comment on Eph. 2:15 ff., Jerome gives first some remarks along the line of what he calls the *vulgatam interpretationem*, i.e., that the Apostle is talking about the breaking down of the wall of division between Jews and Gentiles. But then he goes directly on to state that he who reads these verses in Ephesians while recalling Col. 1:20 will not be satisfied to think that it is Gentile Christians who are said to have been "far off" or that it is the Jews who are said to have been "near" (Eph. 2:17), but will rather suppose that St. Paul here speaks of the joining together of human souls with the angels; the good shepherd has called the sick sheep back to the mountains to be one flock with those on high; man made in the image of God is to receive that *forma* which he once lost and which the angels now possess.[50] It is most difficult to understand Jerome's words in any sense other than that he intends to identify himself with the exegesis here offered. Yet it clearly comes within a hair's breadth of teaching explicitly two points which Jerome was later to denounce. The last of Epiphanius' famous eight points accused Origen of saying that man at the fall had lost the image and likeness of God, and Jerome's words here say virtually if not literally that.[51] We may accept Rufinus' argument on the second point: there appears to be little difference between saying that men will receive the *forma* of the angels, and saying that men will receive the *natura* of the angels, the latter of which Jerome was afterward to find so offensive.[52] The thought that human souls will receive the *forma* of the angels, one might add, is not one that fits easily with Jerome's later insistence upon a "resurrection of flesh and bodily structure," and thus runs against the fifth of the eight points.[53]

It is to be remarked that although Rufinus calls attention to the two passages above, Jerome has nothing to say about them even after receiving the full text of Rufinus' *Apology*. And so one could go on. Jerome seems in the commentary to be quite lacking in distaste for the idea that the devil will be saved and even refers, with no apparent trace of sarcasm, to the one who holds this view as *diligens lector*.[54] But to continue in this vein would be otiose. The noteworthy point is that when Pelagius raised the old charges concerning the commentary on Ephesians, he was hitting Jerome where it really hurt.

One can understand Jerome's anguish. Cavallera, the great biographer of Jerome, wrote in a brief reference of the *singulière illusion* by which Jerome denied the real extent of his following of Origen in the commentary on Ephesians.[55] It was indeed an illusion, but there is something more to be said. Both the integrity of his one consuming interest as a theological scholar and the real nature of his original enthusiasm for Origen were at stake, and on this score one must view Jerome sympathetically. Rufinus and Pelagius, at points thirteen years apart, spurred Jerome to defense of an early and hurriedly composed commentary and thereby contributed to the hardening of a hostile posture which was far from expressing Jerome's real and abiding respect for Origen.

On the one hand, the four Pauline commentaries constituted one of the infrequent interruptions which Jerome had allowed himself in the course of his labors on the Old Testament. He wrote them only at the repeated insistence of Paula and Eustochium, protesting his meager equipment for the task,[56] protesting in the case of Ephesians his own difficulty in understanding the Apostle, and confessing his extensive reliance upon Origen.[57] It is in fact true that in the commentaries of those days he had, to a degree, followed the method whereby excerpts or paraphrases of other commentators were juxtaposed to exegetical remarks of his own—a method apparent, most clearly but not exclusively, in the commentary on Ecclesiastes; this much can be recognized without begging the question of his undoubted sympathy with Origenist views later to become controversial. The unfortunate fact is that in the commentary on Ephesians, Origen at points simply takes over, a phenomenon undoubtedly due to Jerome's enthusiasm for the Alexandrian but also to the circumstances under which the commentary was written.[58]

On the other hand, we may suggest that Jerome's real interest throughout the years of dreary controversy over Origen had not been in identifying himself with the polemic of Epiphanius and Theophilus or in defaming Origen *tout court* but, rather, in seeing to it that no shadow of doubt could be cast upon his own unimpeachable orthodoxy. The evidence assembled by Cavallera is sufficient to demonstrate that Jerome gives explicit and repeated expression to his abiding respect for Origen in the exegetical writings composed in the years between the dying down of polemic in 404 and the appearance of Pelagius on the scene in 414. In fact the same can be said for certain writings which come from the bitter decade 393–404.[59]

There is even some sense to be made of Jerome's repeated assertion, so implausible on the surface, that he had followed and respected Origen not as a teacher of dogma but as an exegete. To accuse Jerome of having accompanied any dogmatic theologian into heresy would have been to misunderstand Jerome's most fundamental theological interest—exegesis of Scripture and in particular of the Old Testament. It was to this end that he gave over so many years of linguistic and textual study and so many years of literary activity. His admiration for Origen was admiration for the most learned, prolific, and ingenious laborer in scriptural exegesis that had yet appeared in the Church.

The challenge from Pelagius in 414 brought on the final freezing of Jerome's hostile stance against Origen.[60] The points outstanding between Jerome and Rufinus after the writing of their two apologies had never approached resolution; Rufinus had simply resumed his other literary labors and refrained from answering when the third book of Jerome's polemical work reached him in 402. Now twelve years later one of the chief of those outstanding issues confronts him again. Pelagius is shooting arrows from the quill of Rufinus. He is, moreover, teaching a doctrine of sinlessness which reminds Jerome (however inaccurately) of Origen; and in support of his teaching he is going about quoting from a book of maxims[61] which Rufinus has translated into Latin and which Jerome is quick to associate with Origenist thought. Pelagius is therefore in the eyes of Jerome not strangely a disciple of Origen and of Rufinus. Pelagius teaches in fact a doctrine to be described as a *nova ex veteri haeresis*.[62]

The charges about the commentary on Ephesians had originally been made in writing by an adversary living as far away as upper Italy. Now they are being made in Jerome's immediate vicinity by an old [63] adversary newly arrived in person. Jerome is as little willing now as ever to have himself implicated in heresy and goes about defending himself with about the same degree of skill as before, i.e., by impugning both the character and the orthodoxy of his accuser. Pelagius is spreading lies about him, and it is in fact Pelagius, not Jerome, who is the follower of Origen.[64]

It is not at all implausible that Pelagius should have arrived in Palestine reproducing charges once leveled by Rufinus.

While no sure evidence is forthcoming that Rufinus and Pelagius knew each other by personal acquaintance, it is quite possible that they had met. A personal encounter could have taken place at any one of two or three different times. One may assume Pelagius to have been resident in Rome from the early 380's until his departure in about 410.[65] Rufinus was at Rome on possibly two different occasions in those years, once certainly in 397–398 and perhaps once in 407–408.[66] We know, moreover, that by August, 410, he was in Sicily, where he was to die; in the preface to his translation of Origen's *Homilies on Numbers* he tells of having been able to watch the burning of Rhegium from across the strait.[67] It would not be surprising that Rufinus, in the company of Roman aristocrats who were also Christian ascetics,[68] should have encountered Pelagius on the island of Sicily. Pelagius was no stranger to such circles of Roman Christian society[69] and was on the island for some period of time before leaving for Africa, where he was in the spring of 411.[70] On Sicily both Pelagius and the circle around Rufinus shared the common status of refugees who had fled Rome before Alaric. But perhaps Pelagius did not meet Rufinus; it could be that he had simply got hold of a copy of Rufinus' *Apology* and had read and noted the sections dealing with Jerome's commentary.

It is not necessary to assume that Pelagius would have been acquainted with Jerome's commentary on Ephesians only at second hand. Pelagius was a reader of Jerome; we know at least that he found Jerome's commentary on Galatians of use in the composition of his own notes on that epistle.[71] It is possible that Pelagius knew of the contents of Jerome's work on Ephesians from his own inspection.

Whatever the manner of Pelagius' acquaintance with this whole issue, one can without danger speculate that he would have been interested in Rufinus' countercharges against Jerome and that he naturally would have been drawn to Rufinus' side of the dispute. Pelagius had already, as early as the year 394, been engaged in polemic against Jerome over the latter's books against Jovinian.[72] But apart from this, Pelagius had particular cause for sympathy with Rufinus in that he had read to his great edification two of the latter's works of translation undertaken on behalf of Latin Christians: the version of Origen's commentary on Romans and the translation of the Sentences of Sextus. Pelagius' use of the latter work will be the subject of the fourth chapter in this book. Some brief comments are perhaps in order on the Origen-Rufinus commentary.

In view of the detailed philological research of A. J. Smith[73] and the theological study of Torgny Bohlin[74] based upon Smith's work, there should be no longer any doubt that Pelagius in his own exegetical work was heavily indebted to the Origen-Rufinus commentary. The commentary on Paul [75] was Pelagius' first literary work of any proportion, and for the composition of this work he found much in Origen-Rufinus which he was able to use for the expression of his own thought. It is not too much to say that Pelagius owed to Origen-Rufinus both the stimulus of important theological ideas and some of the verbal formulae by which those ideas came to expression. This far-reaching influence extends from the important conceptions of *lex naturae* and "grace of creation" through the teachings on baptism and faith to the doctrines of freedom, sin as "habit," and the possibility of sinlessness; and this list is not exhaustive. Of course what is in question here is the influence of "Origen-Rufinus," not pure Origen; it is very doubtful that Pelagius either did or could read Origen in the original. It needs to be said that Pelagius does not simply offer us a shortened version of Origen-Rufinus; as Souter remarked,[76] Pelagius' commentary differs from the other in treating individual verses or clauses rather than groups of verses at once, in his infrequent and restrained use of allegory, and in the relative briefness of his notes as compared to the discursive treatment of Origen-Rufinus. Rather, Pelagius finds a number of ideas and terms in his source which he employs prominently in his own exegesis of particular Pauline passages and which form important parts of what can be called Pelagius' total theological scheme.[77]

The fact of Pelagius' dependence upon Origen-Rufinus merits some reflection. Rufinus' version would not have been available to him before 405–406.[78] Pelagius had by this time lived in Rome for some two decades, and it is most improbable that he was unaware of official actions both papal and imperial that had taken place regarding Origen. Anastasius issued his blanket condemnation of the writings of Origen in 400,[79] and Emperor Honorius at about the same time forbade the reading of his works among Christians.[80] In his fondness for Origen-Rufinus, therefore, Pelagius displays a certain independence of judgment which would clearly have found a kindred spirit in Rufinus of Aquileia.

It has become clear by now that Jerome is not entirely without basis in claiming that Pelagius is a spokesman for both Rufinus and Origen. Pelagius' behavior in raising Rufinus' old charges about Jerome's commentary on Ephesians is to be explained, therefore, rather simply. Faced with charges from Jerome that his teaching on the possibility of sinlessness made him a disciple of Origen, Pelagius was duly reminded of the debt which in fact he did owe to the Alexandrian's commentary on Romans in its Latin version. He adopted the device of defending himself by directing a countercharge against Jerome which had been made originally by Rufinus and which had never been adequately answered.

The picture of Pelagius in Palestine raising old charges against Jerome prompts a further course of reflection. A reconciliation was in process of taking place between Jerome and the party of Rufinus. Three of the company of ascetic aristocrats who had fled Rome to Sicily with Rufinus were now also in Palestine and were there embracing the full monastic life under the eye of Jerome, with whom they were now, it appears, in full affection:[81] the younger Melania, her husband Pinianus, and her mother Albina. This family group had ties to Rufinus through the elder Melania, grandmother to her namesake. The elder Melania had in years before been Rufinus' traveling companion, had presided over a convent on the Mount of Olives in the vicinity of the monastery directed by Rufinus, and had been his continuing friend through the later years in Italy. The grandmother was now dead, although she had been with the younger members of her family and with Rufinus on Sicily. The younger group of three had passed from Sicily to Africa and had there established close relations with Augustine; it was they who were to engage in a late attempt to reconcile Pelagius to the Church,[82] and it was they who from Palestine were to send questions back to Augustine in answer to which the Bishop of Hippo wrote his work on the grace of Christ and original sin.[83] The harmony of this group with Jerome in Palestine stands in contrast to the position there of Pelagius, pressed by the exigencies of controversy into renewing and maintaining an old battle.

It is not surprising that in writing against Pelagian teaching Jerome should concentrate on the idea of sinlessness (understood as ἀπάθεια) and the relation of that idea to the doctrine of God;[84] these were the issues that to him immediately linked Pelagius to Origen. The Pelagian controversy was to Jerome in its most important aspect an extension of the controversy over Origen. In the person of Pelagius, Jerome was confronted with a theological and personal issue which regrettably would not remain in the past.

Something not entirely different can be said of Pelagius as he appeared to Augustine. Again we may refer to Smith's

philological research and to Bohlin's theological analysis
based thereon.[85] In the development of his own thought
Pelagius exploited early writings of St. Augustine, important
among which was the anti-Manichaean work *De libero arbitrio*. Augustine's repeated insistence upon the theological
unity of his thought, from his works against the Manichees
up through the anti-Pelagian treatises, fails to convince.[86]
The Augustine of the greater part of the *De libero arbitrio*
speaks a different language from that of the author of the
De gratia et libero arbitrio. One of the chief theological interests of Pelagius was and remained the combating of Manichaean fatalism.[87] This interest Augustine too once had
taken very seriously, but later subordinated it to his intense
reflection upon the wonder of the divine grace. Pelagius in
fact fastened upon the language of Augustine's early anti-
Manichaean polemic, and integrated it into his own structure of thought. But within Pelagius' structure of thought
the early Augustinian language continued to bear more of
its original meaning than it could within the structure of
Augustine's own mature thought.[88]

In differing ways, therefore, Pelagius appears upon the
scene of controversy in the second decade of the fifth century as a representative to the two great catholic doctors
of still troublesome issues belonging to their own theological
past. To be behind the times was part of Pelagius' lamenta-
ble fate.

In combating the "disciple of Origen," Jerome, on the one
hand, argues in curiously Origenist manner that to be really
without sin would be equivalent to possessing the immutabil-
ity which attaches only to God, and that Pelagius' doctrine
of the possibility of human sinlessness therefore arrogantly
attributes to man the possibility of divine perfection.[89] On
the other hand, Jerome can adopt a somewhat different tack
and say that *in this life* man cannot possibly attain perfection but must await the hour when this mortal shall have put
on immortality and God will be all in all.[90] Sinlessness is
impossible so long as man is in his present bodily state, since

a sinless man would be one who directs his thoughts uninterruptedly to virtue, and to do this is impossible to men whose bodies are continually subject to hunger, thirst, and cold.[91] Jerome obviously and explicitly interprets Pelagius' doctrine of the capacity to be without sin as if it were equivalent to the Greek doctrine of ἀπάθεια, and in this regard he accordingly lumps Pelagius together with Evagruis Ponticus, Origen, and Sextus "the Pythagorean philosopher."[92] Pelagius' rigorism, moreover, in insisting that all the commandments of the divine law are equally binding upon Christians, is nothing but the Stoic doctrine of the equality of sins; it is not the teaching of the Apostles.[93]

Pelagius reacted to such polemic at two levels. At one level he clarified specific points in his own teaching which might not have been altogether clear before the polemic of Jerome forced his attention to them. Thus on the question of the relation between perfection and the future glory, Pelagius now distinguishes two kinds of perfection: one, the perfection possible here and now of obeying all the divine commandments; and the other, the future perfection in which one will no longer be aware of a course still to be finished, a perfection in which one will possess the security of the race already run.[94] Thus Pelagius too can say that in this life there is no "perfection" but mean by this an implied warning that when we begin to stand still, unmindful of the race before us, we have at that moment begun to fall.[95]

Jerome had raised the delicate matter of the relation between sin and the inner motions of mind and thought. Pelagius now makes clear that his doctrine of sinlessness has little in common with the Eastern doctrine of ἀπάθεια. To be sure, sin has its fount and origin in *cogitatio,* and the greatest care is to be taken to extinguish improper thoughts and to nourish the mind with the wholesome delights provided by Scripture.[96] But there is no sin attaching to such improper thoughts as run fleetingly across the mind or to such thoughts as suggest themselves positively but which the will conquers by rejecting them. Only that improper thought is sinful to which the mind gives its consent, desiring that it issue in concrete act.[97]

Concerning the notion of the equality of sins, Jerome had accurately seen that Pelagius placed considerable emphasis upon obedience to all the divine commandments and that he supported this emphasis by quotation of James 2:10: "Whoever keeps the whole law but offends in one point has become guilty of all." [98] Pelagius now, however, asserts that he does not teach the Stoic doctrine of the equality of sins. Sins are distinct in gravity and will be rewarded with differing punishments at the judgment. What he does want to say is that even the smallest offenses are to be feared as if they were the most serious, lest one easily be led on from minor sins to major ones. Besides, all sins whether great or small are committed in contempt of God, and one ought not to consider so much the nature of the commandment as the dignity of the one who commands.[99]

Jerome probably reports accurately Pelagius' response to his first line of argument, stated above; we do not have Pelagius' own words on the subject.[100] According to his antagonist, Pelagius replies quite simply that his doctrine of sinlessness concerns a standard appropriate to the stature of man and not the majesty and perfection of God. The standard in question is that of obedience to the commandments of God, and God who is just does not command the impossible.[101]

Apart from these particular matters Pelagius responded to Jerome at a more profound level. He did this in his two works, De natura and De libero arbitrio. It is of the greatest importance to see the significance of the fact that these defensive treatises were both written in Palestine and reflect Pelagius' proximity to Jerome; De libero arbitrio took the explicit form of a dialogue with that doctor, and De natura bears clear marks also of being written in dialogue form.[102] In writing these works Pelagius sensed accurately that Jerome's greatest theological threat to him did not concern the necessity for the grace made available by the Christian gospel. Jerome was making a fundamental claim about the nature of human existence, whether apart from or in relation to the Christian gospel; he was saying that sin is an inescapable, unavoidable aspect of corporeal existence in this life. It is for this reason that Pelagius' two treatises are so largely taken up with issues related to the doctrine of creation and to the capacity for sinlessness defined in terms of man's created nature. As we shall see in Chapter 6, these matters form one of Pelagius' chief preoccupations in any case, and the teaching of Jerome serves only to heighten this preoccupation. In these works Pelagius says relatively little about the grace of Jesus Christ because between himself and Jerome, as he sees it, that is not primarily the issue.

The issues are rather the relation of man as a creature of God to sin, and the meaning of the idea of sinlessness. When Pelagius, with his attention fixed on these problems, is asked about the role of grace in relation to sinlessness, he not unnaturally takes the step, which he had not heretofore taken, of defining man's capacity to be without sin as itself a gift of grace.[103] With that one stroke he could both assert the peculiar dignity of man as a rational creature and deal with the criticism that his teaching on sinlessness said nothing about grace. But as over against Jerome, his teaching on the capacity to be without sin is a teaching about the nature of man in the context of creation.

In Chapter 5 I shall argue that the first of Pelagius' treatises, when it is read by Augustine, constitutes the real beginning of serious trouble for Pelagius. It is therefore not too fantastic to suggest that the course of events leading to Pelagius' condemnation, in which Augustine played such a prominent role, is in fact an indirect result of the final phase of Jerome's Origenist controversies.

Chapter 3

---◈---

THE CRITIC OF JEROME'S
TEACHING ON MARRIAGE

As THE previous chapter attempted to make clear, there is a relation between Pelagius' revival of charges concerning Jerome's use of Origen, on the one hand, and Pelagius' own literary and theological history on the other. That is, Jerome was not simply talking nonsense in aligning Pelagius with Origen; and Pelagius, in citing Jerome's use of Origen in the commentary on Ephesians, was making a move in his own self-defense. It would not be entirely surprising, then, if something of a parallel sort would be discovered to be the case concerning the second of the charges which Pelagius makes against Jerome in about 414.

Pelagius is of the view that Jerome, in writing his two-volume work against Jovinian, went too far in his depreciation of marriage.[1] What Jerome actually says is that Pelagius "deplores" the fact that in this treatise "virginity is set above marriage, marriage above digamy, and digamy above polygamy." [2]* One is tempted immediately to suspect that Jerome phrases Pelagius' complaint in this way in order to set it in as unfavorable a light as possible, and the suspicion is surely justified. Pelagius, the author only recently of the celebrated

---

* By "digamy" and "polygamy" Jerome means, respectively, remarriage once after being widowed and remarriage after being widowed more than once.

26

letter to Demetrias, cannot with any plausibility be upbraiding Jerome merely for esteeming virginity over marriage.[3] Nor is it at all likely that Pelagius, the author of the Pauline commentary, can be complaining merely that Jerome prefers that widows refrain from remarriage.[4] Pelagius' *Libellus fidei*, sent to Pope Innocent in 417, puts the issue in the terms in which Pelagius undoubtedly saw it: he dissents from the opinion of those who condemn either first or second marriages.[5] In another passage Jerome represents Pelagius as complaining that according to Jerome digamy and trigamy* do not have the authority of divine law but are allowed only by the divine indulgence.[6] Pelagius in fact seems to be singling out for particular attention the matter of the remarriage of widows. Why he should do this is subject for speculation. From scattered references[7] in Jerome it appears that after Pelagius arrived in Palestine he carried on his work of teaching and counseling particularly among women, and it could be that in this context he saw reason to express his disagreement particularly with Jerome's teaching on the remarriage of widows. In such a context Pelagius then engaged not only in an attack upon Jerome but quite possibly in a development of his own views on the subject as well.

This could be seen as follows. When maximum allowance is made for rhetorical excess in Jerome's work against Jovinian, there remains between the position of Jerome and that of Pelagius as found in the Pauline commentary an important difference on the subject of the remarriage of widows.[8] The two authors are at one in their emphatic preference that widows should not remarry and in their view that the Apostle Paul permitted the remarriage of widows in order to save some widows from the worse fate of fornication. Pelagius' comments on 1 Tim. 5:14, however, make it clear that for him it is important that young widows who will likely not persevere successfully as widows should be

---

* Trigamy being three successive marriages, the prior marriages, of course, being dissolved only by the death of one of the partners.

identified as such and that they should marry, since it is a much worse thing, in fact a thing incurring damnation, that a woman should first commit herself to a life of consecrated widowhood only to fall from her promise.[9] It is possible that Pelagius, having arrived in the Holy Land, scene of great enthusiasm for Christian asceticism in its manifold expressions, found a disorderly and to him horrifying situation in which many more consecrated themselves to widowhood than actually persevered in it.[10] He might well then have sharpened his own earlier views on this subject so as to teach that in the case of young widows who are *incontinentes*,[11] remarriage is in fact *de lege*. Jerome's brief remarks in the commentary on Jeremiah suggest such a reconstruction of events. Our conclusion then is that what Jerome tells us about the precise content of Pelagius' charge against him is not *wholly* improbable, although it is in part *most* improbable.

Whatever degree of credibility the above reconstruction of events may possess, there are two points not subject to dispute: that Jerome sees in Pelagius a disciple of Jovinian[12] and that Jerome is aware of Pelagius as a critic of his teaching on marriage as found in the *Adversus Iovinianum*. Of interest about these two points is that they are related to two distinct issues in the teaching of Jovinian—issues not necessarily related to each other, whatever their connection might have been in the mind of Jovinian.[13]

On the one hand, when Jerome accuses Pelagius specifically of being a disciple of Jovinian, he means thereby to align Pelagius' teaching on the possibility of sinlessness with Jovinian's second proposition.[14] The latter in its most basic form states: "Those who with full faith have been born again in baptism cannot be overthrown by the devil."[15] It may be just as tempting to us as it was to Jerome to see in both Jovinian and Pelagius the same kind of perfectionist thought coming to expression in slightly different language. But the temptation is to be resisted. To be sure, one could say that perhaps most of the controversial issues exercising

the Western Church in the latter two decades of the fourth
and the first two decades of the fifth centuries were related
to one large question: the nature of Christian perfection.
One confronts this question in the controversies over Jovinian, Helvidius, Vigilantius, Origen, the Pelagians, the
Manichees, and the Donatists. Jovinian and Pelagius fit
clearly and easily into this general picture, each of them as
it were making a contribution toward the definition of
Christian perfection. Their contributions are nonetheless
rather different. In the case of Jovinian, a *direction* of life
is of chief significance, a direction inaugurated by baptism
with full faith and sustained by the divine indwelling. Such
a direction of life can never be deflected from its final goal
in the kingdom of heaven, not even by the commission of
actual sins, from whose guilt one is restored by *paenitentia*.

It was W. Haller who put forward this interpretation of
Jovinian's second proposition. Although Haller's view means
that Jerome to a great degree misunderstood Jovinian, his
interpretation is sound if only for the reason that, unlike
Jerome, Haller allows us to make sense out of all Jovinian's
language and his use of Scripture.[16]

Pelagius himself has not left us any record of what his
opinion would have been of Jovinian's teaching *understood
in this way*. But one can without difficulty imagine what it
would have been. He would not have disagreed with Julian
of Eclanum, who classed Jovinian, Mani, and Augustine together as sharing the disastrous mistake of denying to the
free movement of the will its decisive importance from
the beginning of the Christian life to its final consumma-
tion.[17] For Pelagius it means nothing to be directed toward
the final goal of Christian life unless that direction is being
continually validated by concrete choices in which the individual wills not to sin. Any doctrine of baptism and of
faith is to be rejected which does not allow that the individual after baptism is continually winning, i.e., meriting, by
works of righteousness that which he does not yet surely
possess—eternal life. Whereas *non posse peccare* can in

Jovinian's thought mean virtually to be without ultimate threat of overthrow by the devil, the phrase to Pelagius would have meant inability to commit concrete acts of disobedience to the divine will.[18] One can imagine Pelagius' dismay that anyone should be identifying Jovinian's teaching with his own. It is not surprising therefore that in the confession of faith which he sent to Pope Innocent in 417 he took pains to denounce "those who assert with Jovinian that man is not able to sin." [19]

On the other hand, Pelagius, in reply to Jerome's charge, seems not content simply to deny such an implausible allegation as that he and Jovinian were of the same mind on "inability to sin." He retorts with a charge of his own concerning Jerome's teaching on marriage. The teaching in question had been directed against Jovinian's first proposition, which declared that no differences in merit attach to the state of the Christian virgin, widow, or married woman.[20] That this subject was for Jerome a troublesome and embarrassing one is clear. Jerome's own friends in Rome had been much upset over the contents of the treatise. Pammachius withdrew copies of it from circulation and addressed a letter to Bethlehem asking the author to defend his views.[21] Domnio copied out offensive passages and sent them to Jerome, asking him to correct or explain them.[22] We need not decide here to what degree Jerome adequately excused himself by suggesting that those who took offense were not aware what kind of treatise it was; he had written γυμναστικῶς, not δογματικῶς and thus in his efforts at all costs to confute his opponent was justified in saying one thing while he meant another.[23] Jerome had in fact described the marital union as malum;[24] had written of the sordes nuptiarum as not being washed away even by the blood of martyrdom;[25] and had suggested that the apostolic injunction to pray constantly could not possibly be followed unless the sexual act never took place, on the ground that sexual union makes one unfit for prayer, according to 1 Cor. 7:5.[26] There was at least some reason for alarm among Jerome's friends.

Pelagius' attack in Palestine on Jerome's books against

Jovinian explains itself by loose analogy with the events discussed in Chapter 2. In both cases we have Jerome associating Pelagius with a discredited figure. There we saw Pelagius attempting to defend his own "Origenism" by the device of raising old charges concerning Jerome and Origen. Here we see Pelagius reacting to the name of Jovinian by again raising an old squabble, this time a squabble in which he himself had been personally involved, and which had indirectly concerned the figure of Jovinian. Pelagius is the unnamed monk of whom we are told in Jerome's letter to Domnio that in about the year 394 he was noisily complaining in Rome about Jerome's treatise against Jovinian and shouting, "Jerome condemns marriage." [27]

It was, I believe, Georges de Plinval who first put forward the suggestion[28] that it is Pelagius who figures in Jerome's fiftieth letter. The suggestion has been taken up tentatively by John Ferguson[29] and without reservation by J. N. L. Myres.[30] It is a point of some historical and theological interest. If the conjecture holds, it will provide us with the one bit of information, apart from his British origin, which we possess about the life and activity of Pelagius in his earlier years, before the turn of the fifth century. It will mean also that before Pelagius turned his interest to theological activity he had been intent upon a career in the law.[31] This in turn will be of some interest in our understanding of key points in Pelagius' theology: the importance which he lays upon the idea of *lex,* for example, or his insistence that God cannot be thought to command the impossible.

I wish to urge the acceptance of the view that the unnamed monk of Jerome's letter to Domnio is Pelagius. To this end I offer below a fuller presentation of relevant evidence than has yet appeared. While it is of course true that the convenience and inherent interest of the hypothesis ought not to push us toward acceptance of inadequate evidence, the skeptic needs also to be warned against the contrary vice of sniffing at evidence only because the hypothesis is convenient.

In the aftermath of the arrival in Rome of Jerome's trea-

tise *Adversus Iovinianum* in 393,[32] an old friend, Domnio,
wrote to Jerome from the capital informing him of the activity of a certain *monachus* who was publicly attacking the
teaching on marriage as found in the treatise. We do not
possess Domnio's letter, but we do have Jerome's reply, in
which he recapitulates much of what Domnio has told him.
We proceed now to a listing of the points of evidence offered
by the letter for identifying the unnamed *monachus* with
Pelagius, taking the evidence for the most part in the order
in which it presents itself in the letter.

   1. The letter describes Jerome's critic as a *monachus* who
is characteristically to be found talking to people on street-
corners and other public places.[33] Pelagius nowhere speaks
of himself as a *monachus* and in fact expresses his opposition to the Latin habit of applying the term to those *in turba
commorantibus;* he is himself of the opinion that the term
is legitimately used among Eastern Christians as applying to
those living in solitude.[34] But in spite of Pelagius' own views
on the proper use of the word, Augustine and Marius Mercator apply the term to him, as do the minutes from the
Synod of Diospolis.[35] Jerome, moreover, elsewhere in a brief
clause opens up a view on Pelagius as a man to be seen
among the people. In the second book of his dialogue, the
orthodox critic asks his opponent (who stands for Pelagius)
how in view of the strict Old Testament prescriptions for
ceremonial cleanliness he can claim any moral purity for
himself—he who is "in the midst of the crowd and a man
of the people." [36]

   2. The monk in the letter to Domnio has as one of his
special concerns the spiritual direction of women. He treats
"mere women" to syllogistic refutations of Jerome's arguments and visits the cells of widows and virgins to lecture
them on Scripture.[37] Concerning Pelagius, Jerome pours
scorn over his dancing attendance upon "mere women" [38]
and goes on to offer an illustrative list of women who have
aided various theological villains in their villainy.[39] With
acid sarcasm Jerome puts into Pelagius' mouth the boast, "I

may be surrounded by hosts of women but I feel no stirring of desire."[40] In similarly trenchant spirit Jerome speaks twice of the "Amazons" who attach themselves to Pelagius.[41] We need not suppose that Jerome is fabricating merely for its potential value as scandal a picture of Pelagius as often in the company of women. It is suggestive that of the five extant letters of Pelagius which we now possess, four are addressed to women.[42] And two of the theses in Pelagius' book of testimonies concern women in particular: "Even women ought to have a knowledge of the law," and "Women also should sing unto God."[43]

3. Jerome in the letter to Domnio contrasts himself, as a student of the two distinguished teachers Didymus and Gregory Nazianzen, to the contentious monk at Rome, "who has achieved perfection without a teacher, an inspired man taught by God."[44] Jerome in 415 makes a comment of precisely this sort about Pelagius—he claims a knowledge of Scripture without having been taught and wants to start out as a master having never been a pupil.[45]

4. From Jerome's letter it is clear that the unnamed monk, although opposing Jerome's teaching on marriage, is himself an opponent of Jovinian; he has "crushed Jovinian in person by the weight of his eloquence."[46] Jerome in the same letter can nonetheless insinuate that the monk is really a follower of Jovinian's teachings.[47] Thus it would not be at all surprising that Jerome some twenty years later and in the heat of controversy should call this monk a *discipulus* of Jovinian, as he does so call Pelagius. Pelagius offers us evidence in writings from his Roman period that he had indeed been opposed at least to certain aspects of Jovinian's teaching. At three places in his Pauline commentary he inserts notes in which Jovinian and the Jovinianists are mentioned by name and in which he records his opposition to the Jovinian teachings that all will receive one reward in the kingdom of heaven and that fasting and bodily mortification are of no value.[48] We therefore know that Pelagius was both critic of Jovinian and critic of Jerome's teaching on marriage in the

Adversus Iovinianum, and we know the same two things about the monk in the letter to Domnio. We know also that Jerome in 414–415 asserted Pelagius to be a *discipulus* of Jovinian, and that he insinuated a similar thing of the monk in 394.

5. Jerome challenges the monk in the letter to let the world know what he is teaching to all those women whom he is seeing in close quarters, to "confess publicly what he says privately." [49] In his letter to Ctesiphon, Jerome remarks of the Pelagian teaching that it is "the only heresy which blushes to say publicly what it does not fear to teach in secret." Jerome charges, "Speak what you believe; preach publicly what you say to your disciples in secret." [50]

6. The monk of the letter to Domnio is a visitor in the houses of noblemen and of ladies of social position.[51] We know of Pelagius' connections at this level of society from his extant letters. The *De lege* is written to a man of senatorial family,[52] and the letter to Demetrias was composed for the daughter of a distinguished Christian noble family at the request of her mother.[53] In the letters *De virginitate* and *Ad Celantiam,* Pelagius finds it appropriate to warn his correspondents against boasting of high birth.[54]

7. Jerome describes his critic of 394 as tenacious in argument and as fighting *obliquo et acuminato . . . capite,* i.e., "with tilted and pointed head." In his dialogue against the Pelagians, Jerome treats his readers to a picture of Pelagius the charismatic leader who, like Moses, has talked with God and who needs no other teacher, a leader going on before us *cornuta fronte,* i.e., with "horned brow." [55] Jerome's words depend in part for their effect upon an interpretation of Exod. 34:29 such that the Hebrew root *qrn* is understood as a noun meaning "horn" rather than a verb meaning "to send out rays," or "to shine"; Moses, then, comes down from Mount Sinai not with a shining countenance but with a horned countenance. This interpretation is found in the Vulgate (*cumque descenderet Moses de Monte Sinai . . . ignorabat quod cornuta esset facies sua ex consortio sermonis*

dei), whence, no doubt, are derived the medieval pictorial representations of Moses with horns on his head.[56] Jerome thus gives the comparison between Pelagius and Moses a nice twist, but a twist that would be without effect if it did not in fact refer to a feature of Pelagius' physiognomy. When to this is added a detail from Orosius, who says that Pelagius "displays his fat even upon his brow," [57] it seems a likely conclusion that there was something noticeably protruded about the man's head. These details about Pelagius from Jerome and Orosius fit together nicely with Jerome's words above about the monk in Rome.

8. A further brief notice on the physical appearance of the unnamed monk corresponds to what we are later told about Pelagius by both Jerome and Orosius. In the letter to Domnio the monk "has the build and the strength of a wrestler and he is nicely *corpulentus*." [58] Writing of Pelagius twenty years later Jerome gives us an unmistakable impression of a man of enormous size whose weight slows him down. He characterizes Pelagius as "towering above with the shoulders of Milo," [59] thus again raising the image of a wrestler. He "plods along at the pace of a turtle," [60] a huge dolt grown wide and thick with Scottish porridge.[61] Pelagius is an Alpine dog, enormous and (again) *corpulentus*.[62] Orosius briefly sketches him as bearing broad shoulders and stout neck.[63]

9. The monk of the letter to Domnio is not a person previously unknown to Jerome. They have met on more than one occasion at gatherings of some sort and have, according to Jerome, argued with each other, in fact have been mutually quite disagreeable.[64] How much credence one should give to the colorful language in which Jerome describes their previous mutual animosity is hard to say, but in any case he knows the man by personal acquaintance, an acquaintance which most probably was made in the years 382–385, when Jerome was in Rome. In the commentary on Jeremiah, Jerome writes, in a discouragingly brief reference, of his "old acquaintance" with Pelagius.[65]

10. In a phrase that may be without significance but then

again may not be, Jerome writes that the unnamed monk discusses "the doctrines of the divine law" with the young ladies whom he is in the habit of visiting.[66] The law of God in both Old and New Testaments is a prominent aspect of the teaching of Pelagius.[67]

11. Jerome wants very much to have a literary controversy with the critic who figures in the letter to Domnio. He wants the man to put pen to paper and so express his criticism in a form in which Jerome can effectively deal with it. The way in which Jerome makes these comments clearly implies that the monk has not yet written anything.[68] This well accords with the facts of Pelagius' literary production so far as they are known. His earliest extant work is the commentary on Paul, which he would not have begun before the year 405.[69]

12. Plinval unearthed the following interesting point. Augustine, composing his long work against Julian of Eclanum in 421, writes of Pelagius that he was not given to saying much in front of others about Jerome, "except for the fact that he envied him as being a rival." [70] Plinval goes too far in suggesting that there is only one likely source for such a comment, viz., Jerome's letter to Domnio. Even if there had been no other written work than that letter from which Augustine could have learned such a thing, he could have received such a report to this effect by word of mouth from travelers coming either from Rome or from Palestine. But it could be, on the other hand, that the source of Augustine's comment is in fact a sentence from this letter of Jerome and that Augustine therefore understood the letter as being about Pelagius. The sentence reads: "Among the women he fancied himself eloquent and of great learning; but when my slight writings [i.e., *Adversus Iovinianum*] reached Rome, he stood in dread of me as of a rival and tried to rob me of my reputation." [71] These words reveal an important aspect of the uneasiness lying behind Jerome's letter. However much the monk sensed Jerome as a rival, it ought to be clear that Jerome had reason to be exercised over the monk as *his* rival. The monk was publicly criticizing Jerome and was

spending his time visiting women—women of high social rank, widows and virgins in their cells—and discoursing to them on the Scriptures. Precisely this had been one of Jerome's principal activities in his years in Rome 382–385 and had gained him some considerable following.[72]

These twelve items taken together, in addition of course to the fact that Pelagius appears in Palestine in 414 as a critic of Jerome's teaching on marriage, give adequate ground for accepting as a working hypothesis the identity of the unnamed monk with Pelagius. The fact that Pelagius' name does not appear in the letter as the name of the monk is of little importance. We may recall that the name "Pelagius" also does not appear in any of the three works in which Jerome tells us most of what we know from him about the great heretic—the letter to Ctesiphon, the dialogue against the Pelagians, and the commentary on Jeremiah. In fact, I believe, the name appears only once in the writings of Jerome, in a late letter[73] to one Riparius, written well after the months of acute controversy and the final papal decision against Pelagius. The absence of Pelagius' name from Jerome's polemical writings against him is probably to be explained by Jerome's reluctance to name an opponent who possessed the undoubted reputation for personal sanctity which we know attached to the person of Pelagius.[74]

We may now say that Pelagius appears at Rome in 394 and in Palestine in 414 as a critic of Jerome's teaching on marriage. This is not without importance to the present state of learned uncertainty over the extant writings of Pelagius. Since 1934 Georges de Plinval has asserted[75] that of a corpus[76] of six Pelagian writings published by C. P. Caspari in 1890, five are to be attributed to Pelagius himself. This judgment has been accepted without question by the author of the only book[77] to have appeared in English on Pelagius in recent decades, as well as by the editor of the recent Migne Supplement.[78] Plinval has not gone unchallenged, however. John Morris has recently called attention to the very questionable grounds upon which Plinval separated the first of the Caspari documents from the other five and has shown that there is at present no reason to doubt that all six come from the same hand.[79] If the six do have one author, he cannot be Pelagius, because the first of the letters contains autobiographical details of a sort not to be reconciled with the life of Pelagius. I have pointed out elsewhere[80] differences between Pelagius' own teaching on marriage and continence and that to be found in the Caspari corpus, and have stated what I take to be the relation properly to be discerned between the writings of Pelagius and those of the Sicilian Briton (as Morris has happily suggested[81] that we call him). One[82] of these six writings bears the title *De castitate*, and it would be very strange indeed if the author of this tract were to be found accusing Jerome of condemning marriage.

We cannot attribute the writings of Caspari's Pelagian corpus to Pelagius himself because the ascetical teaching on marriage and continence to be found in the *De castitate* is not of a piece with the teaching on this subject to be found in the assured writings of Pelagius. It is, on the one hand, quite understandable that Pelagius should have complained about the extremism of Jerome's work against Jovinian, whereas such a complaint would scarcely be comprehensible coming from the author of the *De castitate*. It is the merit of an article[83] by S. Prete to have argued this point in detail. In Pelagius' letter to Demetrias, for example, *iustitia* is the fundamental virtue which properly is common to virgins, widows, and to the married, and continence is clearly described as a *res electionis* and as a state of life *supra mandata;* the Sicilian Briton, on the other hand, posits *castitas* as the *fundamentum . . . sanctitatis atque iustitiae*,[84] and tends markedly toward the view that the ascetic "counsel" of Paul in 1 Cor. 7 has in fact the value of a commandment, on the ground that that which is enjoined upon all Christians is possible only for the unmarried.[85] Whereas Pelagius' letter clearly implies a view of the Christian society in which married persons and virgins both play their proper roles, the point of view of the *De castitate* is that all Christians of serious intent will clearly see themselves summoned to the life of continence, and marriage is only very grudgingly tolerated.[86]

Comparisons in this vein could be multiplied beyond those which Prete specifically draws. On the subject of the nature of incontinence the two authors differ: the more enthusiastic writer expressly opposes the notion that continence is itself a divine gift and posits a decision for incontinence or its opposite as a matter of the "spontaneous will," while Pelagius seems, rather, to regard the personal state of incontinence as one of the facts of life with which one must reckon and in respect of which one must make the appropriate decision.[87]

The Sicilian Briton knew and drew upon Pelagius' commentary,[88] and it will be instructive here to examine a sample passage of the *De castitate* in which the author employs a bit of Pelagius' language but deflects his thought in a radical direction. In question is Paul's statement at 1 Cor. 7:7 that everyone has his own proper gift from God, one in this direction, another in that. Pelagius' comment is confined to six words: *Hoc est propriae voluntatis accepit donativum.*[89] As it stands, the comment is not luminous with clarity, but taken in the context of Pelagius' treatment of the whole of 1 Cor. 7,[90] it suggests that the divine generosity has given to everyone in the matter of marriage and abstaining from marriage the privilege of following his own will, which may go in either direction without fear of opposing the divine will.

The Sicilian Briton writes on the same text as follows: *Propriae scilicet voluntatis, iuxta quam illi non modo nubendi et non nubendi conditio, verum etiam boni et mali, mortis et vitae electis datur, scriptura dicente: "Ante hominem bonum et malum, vita et mors; quod placuerit ei, dabitur illi."* [91] The tendency of these remarks is unmistakable, and it is a tendency away from Pelagius' meaning, although the author introduces his comments by quoting two key words from Pelagius.[92]

It needs to be emphasized that we get a very misleading

picture of Pelagius' teaching on marriage and continence if we rely uncritically upon Souter's text of the Pauline commentary. The subject of marriage is one on which Pelagians show interesting and significant differences, two opposite poles being represented by the Sicilian Briton and by Julian of Eclanum. Pelagius stands somewhere in the middle between these two, and it is not surprising that an early redactor of the text of Pelagius' commentary shows as one of his tendencies to revise in a sense injurious to marriage and sexuality. Dom Celestin Charlier's thesis[93] that Paris MS 653[94] represents the purest available text of the commentary is to my mind worthy of assent. It means for our present subject that in using Souter's text we must pick our way carefully through the comments on 1 Cor. 7 and in particular reject two relatively long passages.[95] In these passages the following ideas are present: that chastity is to be preferred to incontinence on the ground that the former may be possessed perpetually whereas enjoyment of the latter is limited by factors of time, age, and indisposition; that we are not to justify marriage on the basis of Old Testament models, since this might lead us to suppose that various forms of incest are also permissible; that if we really wish to justify marriage on the basis of the command to increase and multiply, we will then confine acts of sexual intercourse to those times when conception is specifically intended; that neither man nor wife may presume upon a partner unwilling to engage in sexual relations; and that in giving direction "not to refuse one another" Paul was considering only the situation in which both partners are *incontinentes,* the instruction not applying to marriages in which one partner decides to be continent.[96]

We may sum up this matter as follows: the whole emphasis of the author of the *De castitate* is to elevate virginity and to depreciate marriage in such a way that it is natural for him to describe marriage as a *suspiciosum bonum*[97] and, following Jerome, to speak of the marital union as a *malum.*[98] Pelagius, on the other hand, so far from merely tolerating marriage, can take occasion in commenting on 1 Tim. 4:2 f.

to insert an unusually long series of remarks opposing every-one *qui nuptias damnat.*[99] Such people really condemn "na-ture" and the created order and are in fact enemies of chastity; their efforts tend to detract from the peculiar merit due to the continent and to encourage fornication by re-moving from the incontinent the remedy of marriage. Now complaint against those who condemn marriage is precisely Pelagius' complaint against Jerome's *Adversus Iovinianum.* Contrariwise, the only regret which the author of the *De castitate* could have had about Jerome's work was that it did not go far enough in its depreciation of marriage.[100]

The conflict of Pelagius and Jerome over marriage and over Pelagius' relation to Jovinian left its mark on the last extant writing which we have from the hand of Pelagius. He sent his *Libellus fidei* to Pope Innocent after receiving the discouraging news in early 417 that the pope had confirmed his condemnation by the African synods. After assuring the pope at very great length of his Trinitarian and Christological orthodoxy, Pelagius comes to issues a bit closer to home. Among the points touched upon are three of Jovinian's fa-mous four theses. As against Jovinian's radical contrasts be-tween righteous and sinners, saved and lost,[101] and as against the denial of degrees of merit[102] and degrees of sin,[103] Pelagius affirms a variety of heavenly rewards and a variety of punish-ments corresponding to varieties of Christian striving and to differing degrees of sin.[104] The Manichaeans err who say that man cannot avoid sin, but just as much do those who say with Jovinian that man cannot sin.[105] And Pelagius abomi-nates those who, with Mani, condemn first marriages and those who, with the Montanists, condemn second marriages.

This last point is a rather nice one. In writing against second marriages in the *Adversus Iovinianum,* Jerome drew upon material which he found in Tertullian's Montanist work, *De monogamia.* The fact may be illustrated from the sections of the two works in which the authors stir the con-sciences of their readers by holding up to view notable pagan figures who abjured second marriages: Dido, queen of Carthage, they both tell us, herself leapt upon the funeral pyre raised to the memory of her husband, Sichaeus, and "preferred to burn rather than to marry." [106] Whether or not Pelagius was aware of the precise literary relation between Jerome and Tertullian, his instinct was sure.

One notable point emerging from this inquiry is worthy of emphasis. The figure of Pelagius first comes into view as an opponent of Jerome's ascetic teaching on marriage. There is a certain symbolic fitness attaching to this fact, for Pelagius was fundamentally a Christian moralist.

Chapter 4

---◄◉►---

PELAGIUS AND THE
SENTENCES OF SEXTUS

I

It was the opinion of Bossuet in the seventeenth century
that heterodoxy may be recognized at once, whenever it appears, simply because it is new. About Pelagius, Augustine
in the fifth century would have agreed. The Bishop of Hippo
held it as a settled conviction that the thought of Pelagius
constituted a radical departure from Catholic Christian
teaching since the time of the Apostles.[1] In an age in which
theological scholarship has become attuned to the mentality
and method of the historian, the question of orthodoxy and
its opposite has become more complex than either Bossuet or
Augustine could consider it to be, although both of them
were in their own times and according to their own lights
historians. Concerning Pelagius in particular, recent scholarship has undertaken to lift him out of his theological isola-
tion and to show lines of continuity between him and Christian thinkers both previous and contemporary with him.[2]
The present chapter is intended as a contribution to this
enterprise.

Certainly one of the most interesting books which Pelagius
included in his theological reading was the enchiridion of
Sextus. We know of his acquaintance with the work from the
fact that in his own book *On Nature* he quoted three maxims

from it by way of supplying support to his position.[3] This of course does not demonstrate that Pelagius was thoroughly familiar with the book or that he drew widely upon it in the formation of his own thought, but it is an invitation to investigation.

The Sextine enchiridion is a collection of maxims which Henry Chadwick has recently brought to attention and made accessible to study by his fine edition of the text accompanied by critical essays.[4] The 451 maxims, largely ethical in concern, have as their author a Christian sage active probably in the late second century and writing in Greek. He had as his kindred spirits the two great Christian Platonists of Alexandria, and Clement more particularly. The sage drew upon a collection or collections of pagan maxims for the most part neo-Pythagorean in provenance. Some of his sayings he apparently left largely as he found them; a great many he modified, usually in a subtle, but unmistakably Christian direction; others he composed himself, and in these there is usually clear evidence of the author's Christian orientation. Two kinds of observation that can be made about the Sentences suggest that their author was engaging in an enterprise of apologetic: on the one hand, pagan maxims are edited, modified, and supplemented to make it clear that a Christian hand has been at work, as, for example, in the opening series of maxims which begins, "A faithful man is an elect man"; on the other hand, Christian material is cast in the form of traditional pagan maxims, and this in such a way that the names neither of Christ, nor of Apostles, nor of any biblical figures are present (this latter fact was later to draw the fire of Jerome[5]). It is as if the sage had been attempting to educate his readers into Christian faith without immediately giving offense over the Christian name.[6]

By the middle of the third century the Sentences had acquired a wide reading public among Christians. Origen informs us at two places[7] in his writings that multitudes of Christians are reading them. Origen himself views the collection as coming from a Christian author[8] and gives his name as Sextus, though with no further identification. The opinion of Origen as to the worth of the Sextine maxims seems to be one of qualified approval. Whereas he speaks of their author as a "wise and believing man" and likes one of the maxims well enough, he says, to quote it often,[9] he nonetheless clearly disapproves of two sentences which give encouragement to enthusiastic Christians wanting to mutilate themselves in the interest of achieving chastity once and for all.[10]

At the turn of the fifth century the maxims have clearly established a high reputation in the Christian community at Rome. They have in fact drawn to themselves the highly honored name of Xystus, Bishop of Rome, whose martyrdom in 258 was intensely remembered by succeeding generations of Roman Christians and whose name to this day stands in the Canon of the Roman Mass.[11] Rufinus of Aquileia tells us of the received belief in Rome that the Sextine maxims have the martyr bishop as their author. As part of his activity of making works of Greek divinity accessible for the edification of Latin Christians, Rufinus translated Sextus for the benefit of a Roman matron of his acquaintance. In the preface to the translation, he states, "I have translated Sextus into Latin, by tradition the same Sextus who among you, i.e., in the city of Rome, is called Xystus, distinguished by his renown as bishop and martyr." [12] While thus not taking responsibility himself for the ascription of authorship to the martyr bishop, Rufinus reports a traditional view, and there is no good reason to doubt his good faith in so reporting a received belief.[13] It was, then, this Latin translation of a work of some second-century Christian sage circulating under the highest auspices which Pelagius quoted in his *De natura*.

In fact Pelagius himself is to be seen as a witness to the traditional ascription to Pope Xystus, although an admittedly interested witness. Augustine informs us in specific terms that Pelagius claimed the martyr bishop as the author of the book from which he quoted, and writing in the last years of his life the Bishop of Hippo observes that when treating

Pelagius' quotations he had mistakenly been of the same opinion concerning their author. Augustine has since learned, he tells us, that the maxims are by the pagan philosopher Sextus.[14] Clearly Pelagius would have read in Rufinus' preface the words about the traditional attribution, and he therefore cannot be claimed as an independent witness. But, on the other hand, Pelagius may be safely presumed to have lived in Rome for some two decades before Rufinus' translation appeared, two decades which for him were undoubtedly marked by intense conversation and exhortation within the Christian community.[15] The traditions of the Church at Rome were not a subject about which he was ignorant. It must be remembered that Pelagius was nothing if not concerned to be a teacher in and of the Catholic Church, as is shown by his numerous polemical references[16] to heretics whom the Church had condemned, by his treatise on the Trinity in which the anti-Arian interest is prominent, and by his notable and unfavorable remarks about the wisdom of "philosophers." [17] At least this much may be said: If the pagan authorship of the Sextine maxims had been as obvious as Jerome was to claim, it is in the highest degree unlikely that Pelagius would have been able to accept the attribution of papal authorship on the sole authority of Rufinus.[18]

It was Jerome who introduced the notion that the Sentences have as their author Sextus, a Pythagorean philosopher, and it is undoubtedly on the basis of having read Jerome that Augustine in his late years makes the same assertion.[19] In the three passages[20] in which he states this view, Jerome's intention is to discredit first Rufinus and then Pelagius: Rufinus with the charge that he has fabricated an absurd claim for the authorship of the treatise which he has translated and wishes to promulgate; Pelagius with the implication that his doctrines of sinlessness and perfection have their origin in pagan philosophical teaching which makes man equal to God and a sharer of the divine substance. It is not to our purpose again to go over the ground covered by

Chadwick in examining the grounds for Jerome's claim and in attempting to ascertain which, if any, Roman philosopher whose name was Sextus, Jerome might have had in mind. Chadwick is surely right in pointing to the essentially polemical and careless nature of Jerome's assertion, is surely right in thinking that we waste our time in searching for the historical figure Sextus Pythagoreus.[21] The only real ground that Jerome can give to his claim of pagan authorship is the obvious one that the name of Christ is absent, as are the names of Apostles, prophets, and patriarchs. This feature of the Sentences can be explained on other grounds, as suggested above. Anyone who studies the maxims carefully and compares them with their pagan parallels[22] and with the New Testament[23] will not find it so easy as did Jerome to suppose that the author of the Sextine collection "did not believe in Christ." [24]

The latter point has been worth making if only because on the theory of pagan authorship the influence of the Sentences of Sextus upon Pelagius would clearly add fuel to the fires of those who, beginning with Jerome and continuing to our own day, have wanted to identify the thought of Pelagius as at bottom pagan.[25] The point is delicate, and one could not deny, would not want to deny, that Jerome's sharp nose has led him unerringly to sniff out the original philosophical environment of the maxims. In language current today, one might say that the Sentences of Sextus are a literary monument to a meeting, an engagement, between Church and world, and one would hesitate today to despise such an enterprise, much less to identify it as evidence of unbelief. Pelagius encountered the maxims in a translated form and encountered them moreover within a shifted intellectual context in the Latin West some two hundred years after their original appearance. Encouraged by the tradition of papal authorship he found in them theological and ascetic materials indubitably Christian and highly congenial to his own mind as he in his context read them. The Greek Christian sage of the late second century contributed in remarkably full measure to the Latin Christian ascetic of the early fifth century.[26]

Before taking leave of Jerome we may notice two further relevant points. He informs us first that the Sextine maxims are "widely read in many provinces."[27] In taking up the Sentences into his armory of theological authorities, Pelagius was making use of a document still popularly read, as in the days of Origen over a century and a half before. Second, Jerome himself encourages us to suppose that Pelagius did not simply dip into the Sentences and strain out from scattered points the three maxims which appear in *De natura*. Rather, one is led to suspect that Sextus has become to Pelagius something like a handbook, ready for repeated use. When Jerome tells us in his commentary on Jeremiah that Sextus is widely read "especially by those who preach freedom from passion and sinless perfection,"[28] he is of course referring to none other than Pelagius and his disciples. In the letter to Ctesiphon he says of the Sentences, addressing Pelagius in person: "Such is the book from which you and your followers quote many passages against the Church."[29] The letter comes from the year 414[30] and therefore probably reflects Jerome's knowledge of the actual practice of Pelagius in addressing Christians after his arrival in the Holy Land.

II

The material which follows will attempt to show that in these assertions Jerome does not mislead. One point must be made clear beforehand, however: it is not being argued that at every point Pelagius derived his teaching either solely or primarily from this one source. That there is a multiplicity of sources contributing to the thought of Pelagius Bohlin has amply demonstrated. There are in fact several places in the writings of Pelagius at which the conclusion seems more than likely that Pelagius had the precise language of the Latin Sextus present to his mind, and I have been able to discover one new explicit quotation from this source. But our more general thesis is that between Pelagius and the Latin Sextus there is a congruence that is unmistakable and significantly wide in range. Pelagius found here a document of Christian piety which in large measure coincided with his own deepest sympathies.[31]

This is evident at the very outset of Sextus as one moves from the first through the fifth and then to the eighth maxim: "The believing man is an elect man; the elect man is a man of God; a man of God is one who is worthy of God; he is worthy of God who does no act unworthy of God; in your eagerness to be a man of faith, see to it that you do no act unworthy of God; he truly believes who does not sin."[32] This quick movement from faith to the notions of action worthy of God and "not sinning" is a movement of thought entirely characteristic of Pelagius and one which becomes particularly visible when he is concerned to make clear that justification by faith does not mean that the Christian is free from obligation to perform "works of righteousness."[33] Pelagius does not linger over definitions of faith, nor does he offer extensive reflections on the phenomenon of faith as such, important though faith is to the total structure of his thought.[34] Rather, he pushes directly to the point that authentic faith leads to works of righteousness. Just as it is clear in Sextus that one who *truly* believes does nothing unworthy of God and does not sin, so Pelagius speaks of those who pretend they have faith which is not joined to works and of "proving" faith by works.[35] It is true that Sextus in these particular maxims speaks in the negative terms of doing nothing unworthy of God and of not sinning, whereas Pelagius in these contexts characteristically uses the positive language of performing works of righteousness; on the other hand Sextus in other maxims not infrequently enjoins positive works,[36] whereas Pelagius can use the concept "not sinning" as an equivalent of *iustitia* and by it refer *tout court* to the whole obligation of the Christian to refrain from that which is prohibited and to perform that which is commanded.[37]

One approaches the Christian life properly, according to

Pelagius, when one recognizes it as one's first and indispensable task to learn what one is to do before attempting to do it. The place where one acquires this knowledge is Scripture (="law," in Pelagius' terms), where the will of God is made known. This theme is the subject of three of the theses[38] extant from Pelagius' *Book of Testimonies*, for one of which he was required to answer at the Synod of Diospolis.[39] It occupies a prominent place in his instructions both to the noble virgin Demetrias[40] and to the young aristocratic Christian to whom the *De lege* is addressed.[41] Although Sextus says nothing explicitly about Scripture, Pelagius will not have missed the import for his own thought of maxim 290: "Learn the things which you ought to do and then do them, so that you do not try to do them before you learn what they are." [42]

Suggestive parallels emerge with respect to general anthropological matters. S 123 reads: "Let the reason which is in you be the very law of your life." [43] In Pelagius reason (*ratio*) has its proper place as the law of life in the sense that *ratio* is virtually an equivalent of that *lex naturae* by which man in the early days of the race was able naturally to acknowledge the Creator and to know the manner in which he should live.[44] It is indifferent to Pelagius whether he says that *ratio* has been clouded over by the long habit of sinning[45] or whether he says that the *lex naturae* has gone into oblivion.[46] Man's permanent vocation is to live according to his own inner nature, which means "to live according to reason and not to be led by the passions of irrational animals," [47] and with this one may compare S 205: "Passion and reason are always enemies in the soul." [48]

Sextus announces a teaching which is strongly reminiscent of Hellenistic philosophy-religion and, appropriately, formulated in the most imprecise terms: "You possess within yourself something similar to God, and because of that in you which is similar to God you are to manage yourself as if you were the temple of God" (no. 35). Beside this may be placed another maxim (no. 398): "If you know by whom

you are made, you have acquired knowledge of yourself." [49]
Pelagius gives evidence of a conception, also not clearly formulated, which allows him to suggest that human "capacity"
to avoid sin is founded upon a divine "capacity" which properly belongs to the nature of God but which God has bestowed upon man as gift of grace. In the *De natura*, Pelagius
observes that the absurdity of the charge that he denies the
grace of God is demonstrated by one simple consideration:
the *posse* of which he speaks belongs not at all to the activity
of human choosing as such but rather to God, the Author of
nature. [50] Later in the *De libero arbitrio* he writes, "*Posse*
is the proper possession of God who has bestowed it upon
his creature." [51] Relevant to these passages and to S 398 is
the remark in the letter to Demetrias, "You ought first to
measure the goodness of human nature by its author, namely
God." Bohlin is certainly right in relating such passages to
the Origen-Rufinus commentary on Romans, which there is
no doubt that Pelagius had studied, and is also right in further suggesting that what began in Origen as man's participa-
tion in Logos has by way of the mediation of Rufinus' translation become Pelagius' doctrine of the capacity to avoid sin,
a doctrine in which *ratio, lex naturae,* and *posse* are all important terms. [52] Our point here is to suggest that Pelagius
could only have read S 35 and 398 with the strongest approval and to direct attention to yet another link between a
pivotal doctrine of Pelagius and the theological environment
of Origen. The movement of thought in S 35, from recognition of the high status of man's nature directly to an ethical
imperative, could scarcely be more characteristic of Pelagius'
bent of mind. And we know that the description of man as a
temple of God which appears in S 35 was congenial to Pelagius, as it appears also in S 46, which he quoted in *De natura*. [53]

A complex of issues related to the foregoing is that which
centers around "knowledge of God" and the relation of this
knowledge to ethical concerns. Two subheadings may be
distinguished.

1. A number of maxims in Sextus give evidence of a hesitation, even a refusal, either to claim speculative knowledge of the nature of God or to talk as if one possessed such knowledge;[54] the knowledge of God of which Sextus does speak is a knowledge bound to man's own proper ethical task, and talk about God is only proper in those who are ethically committed and known to be such.[55] Pelagius disparages the wisdom of "philosophers" who pry into matters obscure and unprofitable[56] and continually specifies knowledge of God as knowledge of God's will, knowledge of the divine commandments.[57] To the noble virgin Demetrias he writes that the highest knowledge that can be recommended to her is that by which one distinguishes vices from virtues.[58]

2. Sextus links knowledge of God closely to "imitation" of God[59] and writes that the highest way of doing honor to God is to make the mind similar to God as far as possible.[60] "Imitating God" for this author would mean, for example, acting toward all men with impartial good will,[61] living without need of things external to the self[62] and without passion in the soul.[63] Pelagius speaks not infrequently in the commentary on Paul of the imitation of God and by it seems to mean particularly the performing of "works of righteousness"; the imitation of God is a particular duty of those who recognize themselves to be sons of God.[64] Pelagius' use of the notion of "imitating God" corresponds therefore to part of the meaning of that idea as found in Sextus, although we shall see below that the idea is not identical in the two authors.

Two particular affirmations about God are to be noticed. (1) S 49 reads, "God is really in need of nothing; the believing man on the other hand is in need only of God."[65] Although the tendency of this remark for Sextus lies in the direction of encouraging the ascetic life, a parallel in Pelagius is not without interest: "God does not need our obedience, but we need his command." The change of emphasis here is suggestive of a significant change of key as between Sextus and Pelagius which will be the subject of brief remarks at the end of this chapter. (2) S 114 announces the proposition, "God is the author of no evil." [66] Such a statement is perhaps not surprising as coming from any Christian author, and surely Augustine would have judged that in his own discussion both on the problem of evil and on original sin he rigidly held to the teaching of this maxim. It is nonetheless important to point out that this teaching constitutes for Pelagius a fundamental axiom of the first importance. It determines the anti-Manichaean tendency which is evident from the first of his writings through the last[67] and in particular underlies the discussions in *De libero arbitrio* of sin as "necessary" and of original sin.[68]

III

A series of conceptions concerning the *general* character of the Christian life show unmistakable parallels.

The immediate basis of ethical striving Pelagius finds in his conception of freedom—freedom to sin, freedom from the "necessity" to sin, freedom to choose the will of God and to obey it.[69] We know that Pelagius looked to Sextus as an authority for this doctrine from his quotation in *De natura* of S 36: "God has granted to men the freedom of their own choice with the undoubted end in view that by living purely and without sin they might become like God." [70] In this maxim the divinely given freedom, on the one hand, and the sinlessness which this gift makes possible, on the other, are closely related ideas. The same holds for Pelagius, as is apparent from a survey of his remarks to be found in *De natura,* in *De libero arbitrio,* and in the letter to Demetrias.[71] Freedom is the divinely given condition of a "spontaneous goodness," [72] implanted in men in order that by their own choosing they may obey the will of God and thus be without sin. In a context in which the center of discussion is that capacity to will either good or evil which God has given to man, Pelagius writes: "When we say that man is able to be without sin, by the very act of confessing that we have *re-*

ceived the ability we are praising God who has bestowed
this capacity upon us." [73]

To be without sin is only what is appropriate to those
who are privileged to be "sons of God." In six[74] of the
maxims Sextus sounds the theme of sonship to God, and in
most of them the verb is in the imperative mood. "One is to
remember in all of one's acts both whose son one is and that
one is a son of God. It is an abomination to call upon God
as Father and to perform a shameful act" (225).[75] Pelagius
chooses one of these six maxims to quote in *De natura:* "A
chaste and sinless man receives from God the imposing
status of being a son of God" (60).[76] The theme of the moral
responsibility of sonship to God is one appearing in Pelagius
a number of times. In the Pauline commentary he remarks
twice that those who call themselves sons of God must imi-
tate the Father in their actions.[77] Once he comments in language reminiscent of Sextus that those whom God has made
sons are therefore to consider whose sons they are.[78] In the
letter on virginity we find him addressing a sentence to the
young lady which in form is similar to a number of the Sextine maxims on the subject and which in fact reproduces a
whole clause from one of them: "Therefore if you are a
daughter of God, see that you do not do any of those things
which are inconsistent with having God as your Father, but
do everything as a daughter of God." [79] And finally to the
noble Demetrias we find Pelagius explaining that there is no
more stringent summons than that by which Scripture calls
us sons of God. "Who would not be ashamed and fearful to
do something unworthy of such a Father?"—a question whose
thought and language both recall Sextus.[80]

We know that Pelagius liked S 46, again because he quoted
it in *De natura:* "A holy mind is a sacred temple for God,
and the best altar for him is a heart pure and sinless." [81] The
association of worship with moral purity appears in pronounced form in Pelagius' letter on the Christian life. The
passage is interesting enough to quote in full here, because
it played a minor role in the course of the controversy over

Pelagius. Jerome singled it out for critical comment in his dialogue.[82] Pelagius was required to answer for it at the Synod of Diospolis,[83] where he denied that the words were his, a denial which we do not have to take seriously, as I have argued elsewhere.[84] The celebrated words are as follows:

> The one who rightly lifts up his hands to God and pours out his prayers with a good conscience is the one who can say, "Thou knowest, Lord, how holy, how innocent, how pure from all deceit, wrong, and robbery are the hands which I stretch forth to thee; how righteous, how spotless and free from all falsehood are the lips with which I pour out my prayers for your mercy upon me." [85]

Sentiments which may be compared to these are to be found in *De lege*, where Pelagius writes of the futility of sacrificial offerings "unless the soul of him who offers be pure and holy"; a defiled heart makes even an unspotted sacrifice unworthy, and obedience to the commandments is more to be desired than any oblation.[86] Here we see Pelagius developing the idea of purity in worship so as to make it include one of his own most characteristic emphases, obedience to divine commandments.

A word of the first importance in Pelagius' ethical vocabulary is *mores*.[87] The development of moral character by beginning and continuing appropriate habits of mind and action is the chief way in which a Christian establishes and tests the reality of his faith. To those leading especially consecrated lives as Christian virgins, the *mores* appropriate to their calling are admittedly difficult of achievement, but it is nonetheless true that success therein is the only way by which their resolution becomes anything more than a name, a word. To Demetrias, Pelagius can formulate the goal for her striving, in preparation for the heavenly reward, as *perfectio morum*.[88] The earlier in life one can begin the development of moral character the better, on the analogy of the training of young plants and animals.[89] Much in accord, therefore, with a prominent concern of Pelagius is S 326: *prout sunt mores tui, talis sit et vita tua; mores enim religiosi faciunt vitam beatam.*

Several of the Sextine maxims display the ascetic concern with integrity of thought (*cogitatio*). That time which is not spent in thought upon God is to be counted as lost; purity of thought as well as of action is to be striven for; one is not to think that sin in thought may be hidden from God: *cogitatio* upon adultery is the equivalent of committing it, and the same is true of every sin.[90] Pelagius took up this theme and in his earlier years was fond of repeating the notion that such virtues as chastity and sobriety are to be possessed "in mind and in body." [91] At a later time he made much more of the matter, writing to Demetrias that *cogitatio* is to be identified as the fount and origin of both good and evil in the soul and that the soul is therefore to be continually on its guard to nourish praiseworthy thoughts and to extinguish bad ones.[92] It is most instructive in this regard to take notice of Jerome's attack upon Pelagius' doctrine of sinlessness. It must be the equivalent, thought Jerome, of the doctrine shared by Evagrius Ponticus and Origen, i.e., that men reach a state of inner imperturbability, free even from all temptation by evil thoughts; in this context Jerome refers with contempt to the Pelagian use of the Sentences of Sextus, which teach the Pythagorean doctrine that man is equal to and of one substance with God.[93] Probably spurred by this kind of criticism,[94] Pelagius in the letter to Demetrias took pains to distinguish among three kinds of evil thoughts: those which merely pass through the mind and which the soul immediately rejects with horror; those with which the soul must struggle and which the will resists and finally conquers; and those finally to which mental assent is given. Only in the third case can evil *cogitatio* be called sin,[95] and this for Pelagius would mean that only the third type merits any serious attention. Thus did Pelagius move away from the outlook of the Sextine author, who could write, "Passion does not arise in the heart of the believing man." [96] In thus moving Pelagius also established his distance in one important respect from those representatives of Eastern perfectionism with whom Jerome had classed him.

In reading the Sextine collection, Pelagius would have come across two successive maxims (388 and 389a), as follows: "Do willingly what is necessary to be done, and by no means do what you ought not to do." [97] One of the most frequently repeated teachings to be found in the writings of Pelagius may represent a recasting of these two maxims considered together under the single heading "righteousness" (*iustitia*). Righteousness is the most general and all-inclusive of the virtues incumbent upon all Christians and consists in two parts: obeying all of the positive commandments in the law of God, and refraining from all that the law prohibits, or more briefly, to do good and to refrain from evil.[98]

In exhorting his readers to conform themselves to the pattern of righteousness, Pelagius usually does not omit some mention of another matter on which he lays considerable emphasis: one is not to suppose that God has issued some commandments which because of their lesser importance may with impunity be ignored. Human evaluations of the gravity of particular divine commands are to be abjured; the Christian is rather to consider the authority, the majesty of Him who commands. Granted that one may speak of the *minima*, one may in no case despise them, and it is very doubtful whether it is possible to speak of such a thing as a "light sin" (*leve peccatum*), since all sin is by definition contempt of God.[99] Four of the Sextine maxims carry a similar theme,[100] and we shall set out the text of two of them below along with some sample clauses from Pelagius so as to display parallels in both thought and vocabulary:

S 9: *etiam in minimis caute age.*
S 297: *non ducas aliud alio peccatum levius.*

Lib. eclog. (Jerome, *Dial. adv. Pel.* 1.32): *ne leviter quidem esse peccandum.*
Cel. 5 (334, 1 f.): . . . *ne secundum divinam sententiam minima contemnendo paulatim decidant.*
Cel. 6 (334, 6): . . . *tamen satis prodesse ad cautionem dicimus etiam minima timere pro maximis.*

Cel. 6 (334, 9 f.): *et sane nescio, an possimus leve aliquod peccatum dicere, quod in dei contemptum admittitur.*

De lege 5 (110, A): *quamquam leve numquam sit, deum etiam in exiqua contemnere, qui non tantum ad qualitatem peccati respicit, sed ad personae contemptum.*

Three of the Sextine maxims assert the priority of deeds over words. The real test of a man is to be found first in his works and only then in his words, and in any case the works of faithful people are to be many, their words few; talk about God only properly comes after deeds in which the divine love is displayed.[101] These sentiments find echoes in the Pauline commentary at places where Pelagius emphasizes that the divine influence moves us first to works and then to words and comments that it is "life" which gives authority to word.[102]

IV

It is instructive to notice parallels concerning *particular* matters in the proper governing of the Christian life.

Sex is a subject very much in view in the Sextine maxims. Overlooking differences in detail we may see a similarity in the basic shape of the teaching on sex in the two authors. Whereas Sextus, on the one hand, clearly regards sexual desire as a block to the soul's intimacy with God and sees continence as a proper goal for all to pursue even within marriage, where partners are to rival each other in striving after continence, he, on the other hand, gives explicit approval to marriage and the procreation of children for those who are aware of the grave responsibility involved.[103] In Pelagius a similar tension is evident. Continence is clearly to be desired over its opposite;[104] those who have undertaken lives of consecrated virginity have chosen a higher life leading to a higher heavenly reward;[105] partners practicing continence within marriage are described as *perfecti*.[106] But Pelagius wishes also to make it clear that marriage is an entirely acceptable state and that those who enter upon it and maintain sexual relations are by no means to be disparaged. This side of Pelagius' teaching is clear from his exegesis of 1 Cor. 7,[107] from his advice to the matron Celantia,[108] and from his opposition to Jerome's treatise against Jovinian, which we discussed in Chapter 3. The chief differences between the teachings on sex and marriage of Sextus and Pelagius are three: (1) whereas Sextus sees the proper ground of permissible marriage as courage to undertake a challenging responsibility and will allow nothing to be done *"propter solam libidinem,"* Pelagius recognizes sexual desire as legitimate reason for marriage;[109] (2) Sextus allows self-castration to those unable to control sexual desire,[110] while there is in Pelagius no word about this possibility;[111] (3) Sextus would seem to permit one married partner to renounce the marriage bed in order to live in continuous union with God,[112] whereas Pelagius rebukes Celantia for having done precisely that without having reached a mutual agreement on the matter with her husband.[113] Finally, Sextus in two maxims places sex and the belly together as twin threats to the life of the sage; it is necessary to keep the strictest control over both sorts of desire.[114] Pelagius writes to Demetrias that the two voices which are chiefly responsible for leading men astray are *gula* and *libido*.[115]

On the proper attitude to the goods of this world five items may be distinguished, all of which display parallels, and one of which finds Pelagius offering a hitherto unrecognized quotation from Sextus. (1) No steps are to be taken to save one's property from imminent theft. One of the headings from Pelagius' book of testimonies reads: "A Christian ought to be possessed of such forbearance that if anyone wants to rob him of his goods, he gladly lets them go." [116] S 15 instructs in the same manner: "Even if someone robs you of whatever worldly goods you possess, do not be angry." [117] (2) In obviously Stoic vein a number of the maxims instruct that one is to strive to possess only that which can be permanently kept and which no one can take away.[118] The theme appears in Pelagius a number of times,[119] and he takes the trouble to cite examples of not uncommon human behavior whose absurdity he is trying to point out: men willing to fight with beasts for gold which they cannot possess in eternity,[120] men who, contracting a light fever after overindulgence in food and drink, are willing to promise almost all their worldly goods to a physician able to cure them for a life which will one day come to an end.[121] Pelagius' employment of the theme is much more obviously biblical and eschatological than that of Sextus; the passing away of all things he associates with the final woes and the judgment, and that which *can* be permanently possessed is the reward of eternal life. (3) According to both authors one is to possess only as great a portion of the world's goods as is "necessary." [122] (4) Both authors lay firm emphasis upon the duty to distribute one's goods to the poor. This is the theme of no less than nine[123] of the Sextine maxims. Pelagius devotes an unusually long paragraph to this subject, for example, as he comments on 1 Cor. 13:3,[124] and elsewhere describes the dominical summons to "go, sell" (Matt. 19:21) as the "basis of perfection." [125] (5) Sextus announces[126] the doctrine that those who have one God and Father in common ought therefore to have all earthly possessions in common. In commenting on 1 Cor. 12:13, Pelagius writes that those who have spiritual things in common "ought to possess carnal things in common"—

secundum sententiam viri sapientis et sancti qui dixit, *quorum unus est deus idemque pater eorum nisi et possessio communis est impii sunt.*[127]

Pelagius quotes S 228, and we thus have evidence that he was acquainted with and approved of the Sextine author as early as the writing of the Pauline commentary, i.e., before 410.[128]

Three maxims from Sextus deal with the topics of ruling, judging, and being judged. He who is set over men is to remember that God is set over him; one who judges men must know that he will be judged by God; there is greater danger to the judge than to him who is being judged.[129] These themes find parallels in Pelagius and in particular in the third chapter of the letter on Christian life. There the fate of unthinking magistrates is painted in dark tones in such a way that the whole discussion can be seen as offering exemplification of Sextus' three maxims. The more power, the more temptation to sin. Magistrates who do not fear the judgment of God have this judgment visited upon them as a result of their cruel and unjust sentences; their own fate as they lie unburied, food for vultures, is more degrading than that of the innocent victims whom they have condemned to death.[130]

There remain a number of more minute matters, which in the light of the above material serve to fill out the picture. Pelagius has recurring remarks much in the spirit of some of the Sextine maxims on the following subjects: possessing virtues in fact and in appearance,[131] disparaging others,[132] flattery,[133] being careful to whom you lend your ear,[134] and intercessory prayer.[135]

Finally one cannot ignore the fact that one of the Sextine maxims announces the final judgment as bringing with it unending rewards and unending punishments.[136] There is scarcely a single motif more characteristic of the writings of Pelagius.[137]

V

It would be a mistake to leave the impression that the teaching of Sextus considered as a whole is simply commensurate with the outlook of Pelagius. Some brief remarks are therefore in order about important contrasts between them, although a full discussion of this matter would take us into far corners beyond our interest here.

The most fundamental, most comprehensive contrast between them is one that centers on the basic image of man and of man's relation to the divine. It must of course be remembered that the Sextine book, consisting in discrete maxims, has no connected prose writing in it and that by far the greater number of the maxims have a specifically ethical direction; any attempt to supply a philosophical context of thought must therefore be somewhat speculative. It would appear certain however that the Sextine author speaks against the philosophical background of a cosmic hierarchy of being. The soul of the sage is lifted up to a status in this hierarchy just under that of God. He is repeatedly said to be "next to God"; he is a "mirror of God," the "image of the living God"; he has that freedom over the world which is properly that of God and "possesses" all that God possesses. The "first" being in the cosmos is God, the "second" the man who is receiver of the divine favor.[138] There is in man "something similar" to God.[139] The incontinent man defiles God himself.[140] The soul of the pious man is "God among men" (it is significant that of the three maxims which assert this particular doctrine, Rufinus omitted two of these in his translation).[141]

It is more than doubtful that Pelagius either had any grasp of this basic context of thought or understood individual maxims giving expression to it in anything approaching their original meaning. He on the contrary saw all Christians most fundamentally as under obligation to obey the commandments of a just and righteous God and some Christians as choosing to take upon themselves the higher summons to chastity and contempt of the world. Both kinds of Christian are empowered toward their goal by the basic structure of human nature as having implanted within it *ratio, lex naturae,* a gift of God. To be sure this conception was in part derived from a middle or neo-Platonic context of thought, as Pelagius' dependence upon Origen-Rufinus clearly shows, but this derivation was mediated by the filter of Rufinus' version and it would be a mistake to suppose that Pelagius had any appreciation of the total context of Origen's thought. Pelagius, rather, extracted ideas suggested to him by his Latin sources in such a way that *ratio, lex naturae* and *conscientia* are joined together in a transformed conception. By the way in which God has constituted human nature man is free from the "necessity" of nature to lead a life in accordance with rational divine will; to say that man may live in accordance with his own nature is one way of saying that man may obey the divine will, and this in its turn means doing certain kinds of acts and not doing others. It is true that Pelagius seems to aver that man and God are at one in a crucial way, which he states rather simply and naïvely: both man and God "are able" to be without sin, God possessing this attribute in his own "nature" and man by gift of grace. But man as obedient to his Lord is the dominant image for Pelagius, not man as lifted to participate in the divine abstraction from the world.

On the basis of this fundamental contrast one can understand some further subsidiary ones. Whereas the imitation of God in Sextus carries with it all the ontological implications of freedom from passion, freedom over the world, "possession" of the world, this notion in Pelagius means really imitation of the divine acts of righteousness. God as in need of nothing and the believing man as in need only of God would naturally be transposed in Pelagius into the notion that God does not need our obedience but that man's chief need is of obedience to the divine command. The presence of the words *sapiens* and *sapientia* in the Sextine maxims[142] probably contributes to the frequent appearance[143] of these words in Pelagius, who can indeed speak of wisdom as "the mother of all virtues." [144] But for Pelagius the wise man is not the sage who has been elevated to the secondmost peak of the cosmic hierarchy where he participates in the divine independence of the world; he is, rather, the man who knows the Scriptures, and has learned from them to contemplate the passing away of all things temporal.[145] Whereas it is not surprising to find in Sextus the statement, "Nothing good comes from the flesh," [146] and not at all difficult to fit such a doctrine into a neo-Pythagorean or neo-Platonist context, Pelagius on the other hand labors to explain that St. Paul's negative assertions about "flesh" do not refer to any evil "substance" which God may be thought to have created but that rather the Apostle was talking about "fleshly habit" under whose power men have allowed themselves to fall.[147]

And finally, a matter of some interest. We noted above that Pelagius quoted S 36 as expressing and supporting his own doctrine of free will. The Greek original of S 36 and Rufinus' Latin version are to be translated, respectively, as follows:

> God has given to the believing man a freedom [ἐξουσίαν] which is divine and therefore pure and without sin.

> God has granted to men the freedom of their own choice [libertatem arbitrii sui] with the undoubted end in view that by living purely and without sin they might become like God.[148]

Origen, in the second book of his commentary on John, provides a helpful clue to the meaning of the Greek:

> There are among the Greeks certain teachings, called paradoxes, which, accompanied by a kind of proof or apparent proof, attribute the highest conceivable dignities to the man who in their view is a sage. Accordingly, they say that the sage alone and every sage is a priest, because the sage alone and every sage possesses knowledge as to the service of God. And they say that the sage alone and every sage is free in that he has received from the divine law the freedom for independent action [ἐξουσίαν αὐτοπραγίας]; this freedom they define as a lawful power of decision.[149]

In a passage from Diogenes Laertius' account[150] of the Stoics, we find terms which correspond precisely to key words in the lines from Origen above. After reporting that the Stoic teachers encourage following the Cynics and assert that even the eating of human flesh is permissible if the circumstances indicate it, Diogenes goes on to record the teaching that only the sage is free, and that freedom means "freedom for independent action" (ἐξουσίαν αὐτοπραγίας). We have, then, a Stoic tradition which sanctions for the sage his own freedom of unfettered action and which, as reported by both Origen and Diogenes Laertius, employs to denote this freedom the twofold term ἐξουσία αὐτοπραγίας.

A link between this Stoic tradition and Sextus is provided for us by Porphyry. Among the aphorisms which that philosopher set down in the celebrated letter to his wife Marcella is the following: "God has given to the sage the freedom of God." [151] Chadwick has made it clear beyond doubt that both Sextus and Porphyry drew, independently, upon a prior pagan collection of aphorisms.[152] In attributing "freedom" to "the believing man" Sextus has followed his practice at many points and has revised in a Christian direction a pagan original, an original which in this case had attributed such freedom to the sage. From both Origen and Porphyry we may gather that in the tradition of this whole idea was the notion that the authority or freedom bestowed is "divine" in some sense; according to Origen it is an authority received "from the divine law," whereas Porphyry speaks simply of θεοῦ . . . ἐξουσίαν, which could either mean a freedom or authority attaching to God himself or simply authority "from God." Sextus interprets this notion to mean that the autonomous freedom or authority which is bestowed is one which is proper to God and is therefore by definition pure and without sin, just as is God. By this, Sextus would presumably imply that actions undertaken by the believing man in accord with his high license are also pure and without sin.

Rufinus in his translation works three notable changes from the meaning of the original: (1) The idea of a freedom or authority for autonomous action is replaced by the Latin idea of freedom of choice. Thus with one fell swoop does Rufinus introduce into the text of Sextus a problem which was gathering momentum in Western theological writing but which was absent from the original Greek. (2) This freedom is bestowed upon "men," not upon "the believing man," much less upon the sage. (3) Purity, sinlessness, and likeness to God now become goals which are possible upon the proper use of freedom of choice rather than properties of the believing man's autonomy of unfettered action.

Through the distorting mediation of Rufinus, then, was Pelagius encouraged to suppose that he had found, in a precise maxim of the martyr Bishop of Rome, authority for one of his most cherished teachings.

Chapter 5

———<❮◉❯>———

ON AUGUSTINE AND PELAGIUS

PELAGIUS is one of the most maligned figures in the history of Christianity. It has been the common sport of the theologian and the historian of theology to set him up as a symbolic bad man and to heap upon him accusations which often tell us more about the theological perspective of the accuser than about Pelagius. The great heretic has had a peculiar way of raising to the surface the theological preoccupations of his detractors and of bringing these preoccupations to tendentious and hostile expression. The two great orthodox doctors who wrote against him in his lifetime attack him with noticeably different emphases. To Augustine he is the enemy of the grace of God; he has made the cross of Christ to no effect; he has introduced novelty and heresy in his denial of original sin.[1] To Jerome he is the continuer of the perfectionism of Origen;[2] his doctrine of sinlessness brings with it the absurd and blasphemous claim that man may be made equal to God.[3] The testimony of Augustine is instructive in this regard. Not having read Jerome on the subject, the Bishop of Hippo registers surprise and dismay when he learns that certain persons are attacking Pelagius on the ground that to be without sin means to be equal to God.[4]

In our own century the name of Pelagius has remained a constant target. Karl Barth will have us believe that Pelagius sets out a doctrine of man's own self-determination in the place of a proper doctrine of man's being determined by God. Pelagianism represents the survival of a "heathen atavism" within a Christian doctrine of God and posits an absorption of the Godhead into the personal will of the created individual; it ascribes to the human will an autonomy in relation to God's will which the human will cannot possess because its freedom is only relative.[5] In the Diekamp-Jüssen handbook of Catholic theology we find that it is one of the marks of Pelagian theology to deny that man in his original state was equipped with grace.[6] This is surely a surprising judgment in view of one of Augustine's chief complaints against Pelagius, viz., that when he set out to discuss grace he spoke only of that grace given to man's original nature at creation.[7] M. Schmaus levels the not uncommon charge that in the thought of Pelagius Christ benefits humanity only by his good example and thus that there is no real theology of redemption.[8] On this point Pelagius has even been placed alongside the Socinians as exchanging a proper theology of the cross for a doctrine of "example." [9]

On the side of the historians we may single out Harnack as offering extreme and yet influential judgments. For Harnack the basic issues in the Pelagian controversy are those of virtue as opposed to grace, morality as opposed to religion, the original and unlosable ability of man as against the power of Jesus Christ.[10] Pelagian theology is to be characterized as a "rationalistic moralism." [11] Implicit within this theology is the denial of any doctrine that cannot be defended by reason, and with this working principle did the Pelagians perform their exegesis, willfully attempting to bring Scripture into accord with their beliefs.[12] Harnack incorrectly attributes[13] to Pelagius the assertion that "all men whom God creates are in the same condition as was Adam before the fall." Pelagian teaching knows and wants to know nothing of salvation and is *"im tiefsten Grunde gottlos."* [14] Finally, Harnack purports to quote from Pelagius' letter to Demetrias a sentence which reads, "Nature is created so good that it is in need of no help." [15] The sentence stands nowhere in that letter nor in any other extant writing or fragment from Pelagius.

In the foregoing selection of ancient and modern charges

against Pelagius are to be found assertions of at least three sorts: (1) factual assertions, i.e., that Pelagius did or did not hold certain precise views, such as that all men created now are in the same state as Adam before the fall; (2) evaluative assertions, such as that Pelagian theology is fundamentally Godless; (3) assertions which in some proportion are a combination of types 1 and 2, such as that Pelagius has no real theology of redemption. Not everyone who writes about Pelagius does so in a hostile and tendentious way, and some studies in recent decades have gone far toward creating a climate of scholarship in which it will be more and more difficult for knowledgeable writers either to level false accusations of fact or to make evaluative judgments which are at best misleading. Thus, Jean Rivière in an exhaustive article[16] has called attention to Pelagius' repeated emphasis upon the death of Christ as an unmerited sacrificial offering for the sins of men as well as to his doctrine of free, gratuitous justification made available to the man of faith through baptism. The burden of proof must now rest upon the critic who still wants to say, "Pelagius really didn't mean it." Attempts to establish a critical text of Pelagius' commentary on Paul [17] as well as to settle the question of the number and identity of Pelagius' extant writings[18] have been of obvious importance in establishing the factual content of his teaching. Also of help toward this end has been the growing awareness that one must distinguish among Pelagians, that it is no longer profitable to write short, summary essays which synthesize the positions of such disparate figures as Pelagius, Celestius, and Julian of Eclanum. And finally, the important monograph[19] of Torgny Bohlin has performed two useful services: it has developed extensively the thesis that the basic direction of Pelagius' theology is anti-Manichaean and has exposed significant lines of theological continuity and literary dependence linking Pelagius to Christian theologians both antecedent and contemporary with him. Bohlin's book has now made quite otiose such an evaluation as that Pelagius' theology is at bottom Godless.

Undoubtedly the chief single reason for the recurring polemic against the name of Pelagius is the continuing influence of St. Augustine in both Catholic and Protestant theology. This is not meant to suggest that modern critics of Pelagius normally assume an uncritical stance in respect of Augustine; there are in evidence today few proponents of an undiluted Augustinianism. But many a writer would seem to hold at least implicitly that Augustine perceived the real danger posed to Christian theology by Pelagius and offered arguments against him which in that theological context were on the right track, even if one would now want to formulate the doctrines of sin and grace in different terms. St. Augustine remains the honored doctor of grace.

For those of Catholic commitment it may remain of importance that Pelagius was condemned by the first Council of Ephesus in 431 and by two popes, Innocent I and Zosimus. But even in this regard the figure of Augustine looms large. The action of the Council of Ephesus was a recognition and reaffirmation of previous papal actions;[20] Cyril of Alexandria, president of the council, knew little of a precise nature about Pelagius and was inclined to use the issue of Pelagianism as a weapon by which to alarm the papacy over Nestorius.[21] The papal actions themselves, so far as they were theologically motivated, were undertaken in the first instance through the initiative of African bishops whose theological spokesman was Augustine of Hippo.[22]

That facet, then, of the fifth-century controversy over Pelagius which to this day has retained theological importance is that in which we see Augustine faced against Pelagius. Now there are at least two ways in which to study this facet of the controversy: to compare the doctrines or to follow the concrete historical events. One may, on the one hand, gain a comprehensive view by synthesizing all the relevant passages from the two writers on the subjects of sin, grace, and freedom and set side by side for comparison the two positions thus synthesized. An extension of this method, bringing more interesting results, would be to juxtapose the total theologies of the two figures, and in doing so to pay particular attention to such matters as basic intention and direction of thought, and the relation of theological formulations to philosophical conceptions and terms current in the early fifth century. This line of approach is of unquestioned value, and one might even concede the point that along this path are to be sought the results of most lasting theological significance. But if used exclusively, this procedure has two serious shortcomings, one general and one specific. First, the comparison of systems of thought involves an abstraction from the actual course of events. In theological controversies it is not in the first instance systems of thought which "confront" each other, but men—men who speak and write on concrete occasions, men whose thought may be in flux and may be bent by the very events of controversy in which they are participating. Abstraction here inevitably brings with it some measure of distortion. Second, the controversy over Pelagius in particular follows an interesting and odd course. It is to this peculiar course of events that we now wish to turn attention. We wish to begin a quest for the historical controversy over Pelagius, and we do this in the sure and certain confidence that the actual, historical course of the controversy will not be irrelevant to whatever judgment one may finally want to make about the contrasting theologies of Pelagius and Augustine.

The course of the controversy suggests the following intriguing question: At what point does "the Pelagian controversy" become specifically a controversy over Pelagius? [23] Answer: at that point in the year 415 when Augustine writes his work *On Nature and Grace* in response to Pelagius' work *On Nature*. To justify and to point to the implications of this answer will occupy us for the remainder of this chapter. A similar question and a like answer were posed over sixty years ago by Friedrich Loofs in his encyclopedia article[24] on the Pelagian controversy, an article which to this day remains the best single survey of the subject.[25] Loofs made his point in a rather brief way, and it is proposed in the following to substantiate, to extend, and to qualify the position which he stated then with admirable clarity and directness.

It might be objected at the outset that the controversy really began at that famous moment in Rome sometime during the first decade of the century when Pelagius was listening to a bishop read from Augustine's *Confessions*. According to Augustine's report, Pelagius raised emphatic objection when he heard the words, "Give what thou commandest, and command what thou willest." [26] But this incident does not affect our thesis. For though Pelagius may not have liked what he heard from the *Confessions*, he cannot be thought at this time to have been a theological opponent of Augustine. As we now know, Pelagius was finding much of which to approve in more than one work of Augustine's[27] and was later to quote Augustine in support of his own position.[28] In any case our chief concern is with Augustine's opposition to Pelagius, not *vice versa*. Augustine's report of the incident in Rome appears in a late work from the years 428/429, and there is no sure evidence in his writings through the year 415 that he knew of such an incident.

The work *On Nature and Grace* is usually thought as being, in chronological sequence, the third in the group of writings classed as Augustine's "Anti-Pelagian Treatises." There is nothing really with which to quarrel in this classification, so long as one understands "Anti-Pelagian" in a broad sense. But one must read with a certain care the remarks with which in 427 Augustine would recall the writing of the first of these treatises. "The necessity arose," he would write, "which compelled me to write against the Pelagian heresy." [29] It is understandable that at a distance of fifteen years the author should have used an adjective made from the name "Pelagius" in describing the heresy; he then regarded Pelagius as the central figure against whom he had written from the outset.[30]

The first treatise, *On the Merits and Forgiveness of Sins*, is not in fact directed against Pelagius. Augustine addresses the work in 412 to his acquaintance the tribune Flavius

Marcellinus, who, in the previous year, on imperial appointment, had presided over the important meetings in Carthage between Catholics and Donatists. This Marcellinus has written a troubled letter to Augustine telling the bishop how he is being wearied by disputes with certain persons at Carthage and asking for advice. Many of the weak brethren are being upset.[31] Augustine takes up in the first two books of his work the chief points of contention as reported by Marcellinus. These several points are in some cases identical and in others closely related to the theses condemned in the year before by a Carthaginian synod at which Celestius was under interrogation.[32] The synod had not had the effect of settling the disputed points at Carthage; discussion and development of the theses had proceeded apace. Pelagius, having been at Carthage in June of 411, had shortly thereafter sailed for Palestine[33] and was in the African city neither at the time of the synod nor during the ensuing months of discussion. Neither his name nor the name of Celestius is mentioned in the first two books of the work, nor, apparently, is any writing from either of them quoted. Augustine writes against views held by Carthaginian Christians, views related to the six theses which Celestius had refused to condemn.

Our point is not at all to suggest that Pelagius would have wanted to dissociate himself from all the views discussed in the first two books of the work *On the Merits and Forgiveness of Sins*. With some of them he would have agreed: that there were sinless men before the coming of Christ,[34] that sin is not transmitted from parent to infant,[35] that unbaptized infants who die are not subject to condemnation.[36] From one of them he certainly would have dissented: that Adam would have died a natural death even if he had not sinned.[37]

At the beginning of the third book, Augustine introduces the name of Pelagius. He has within the last few days read Pelagius' commentary on the Pauline epistles, and there he he has found, he reports, in the comments on Rom. 5:12[38] some arguments against the doctrine of original sin. The arguments may be paraphrased as follows: (1) if the sin of Adam harms even those not guilty of actual sins, i.e., infants, then the righteousness of Christ must be thought to benefit even nonbelievers, since the Apostle Paul argues that salvation is brought through one man in a similar, even greater way, than death has been brought by one man; (2) if original sin is cleansed away by baptism, then the offspring of two baptized parents can scarcely inherit what their parents no longer possess; (3) on the assumption that only bodily nature is inherited and that soul is not inherited, bodily nature alone would presumably be afflicted with inherited sin and thus deserving of punishment, and in any case it would be unjust that a newly created soul should have to bear the weight of a sin committed so long ago and by some other person; (4) it cannot be believed that the same God who forgives a man his own sins should reckon against a man the sin of another.[39]

These arguments Augustine wants strongly to contest. He is careful to note, however, that Pelagius does not introduce the arguments as opinions of his own; they are arguments of "those who are against the idea of transmitted sin." [40] Thus while taking strong issue with a passage found in Pelagius' book and while sure that such opinions represent "novelty," as opposed to the opinion implanted in the Church since antiquity,[41] Augustine at the same time speaks of Pelagius himself in terms of high respect. He understands from reports that Pelagius is a "holy man," a man "who has made no small progress in the Christian life." [42] The bishop is able to persuade himself that "so distinguished a Christian" could not give his approval to arguments so "perverse and repugnant to Christian truth." [43] Is Augustine indulging in sarcasm? Certainly not sarcasm of the sort enjoyed by Jerome. To anticipate a bit, let us say that he is deliberately choosing to read Pelagius *in meliorem partem*, and this for the reason that Pelagius has such an undoubted reputation for personal sanctity. By the evasive manner of introducing his comments, Pelagius has provided Augustine with an easy opportunity to contest the views while paying tribute to the man.

The second of the "Anti-Pelagian Treatises" is that *On the Spirit and the Letter,* the most attractive and compelling of all Augustine's works related to the controversy. Addressed to the same Marcellinus, it begins as an answer to a question which arose out of the first treatise. Marcellinus was puzzled; Augustine had written that while one must admit the possibility that a man may be without sin if aided by the grace of God, one must nonetheless say that in fact no sinless man in this life has ever lived or is likely to live except the one Mediator Jesus Christ.[44] From consideration of this point, Augustine in the treatise very quickly broadens the discussion into a general treatment of the antithesis between law and grace, taking as his chief text the Pauline verse, "The letter kills but the Spirit gives life." The tone of the treatise is noticeably irenic. The author is not even willing at this juncture to press his opinion against those who assert that a sinless life here is possible. Those of this view hold no dangerous error.[45] But the point that Augustine must make with the greatest insistence is that they are wrong who suppose that men may either attain or progress toward perfection through the exercise of free will in obedience to divine commandments.[46] The law of God which is merely heard and read is the letter that kills; the law of God written upon the heart and stirring the will to cleave to its maker is on the contrary the work of the life-giving Spirit.

There is in the treatise *On the Spirit and the Letter* no mention of Pelagius or of any other specific persons whom Augustine may have in mind as holding erroneous doctrine. At at least two points in the work, however, one should most probably see criticism of particular doctrines of Pelagius. Augustine has now read Pelagius' Pauline commentary[47] and is presumably aware of the repeated teaching there that law and commandment are to be prized as offering knowl-

edge of the divine will and are thus to be understood as
"grace";[48] he is presumably aware also of the prominent
teaching on free will;[49] and he cannot have failed to notice
that a conception of grace, in anything approaching his own
distinctive sense, is virtually absent. So when he warns
against those who say that God's "help" consists in his giving us knowledge of his commandments, to which we may
respond in the freedom of our own will, he is probably
arguing against Pelagius.[50] The same thing is likely when
Augustine comes to discuss the Pauline conception of the
"law by which no man is justified." Pelagius at several points
in his commentary expresses the view that the law apart
from which man is justified is the ceremonial law of circumcision, Sabbath observance, and the like. Such a notion is the
precise target of criticism in one section of Augustine's.
book.[51] It is in particular, then, the two ideas of the law
as "help" and of the law-that-does-not-justify as ceremonial
law which make it likely that in the work *On the Spirit and*
the Letter Augustine is at least in part dealing with teachings which he has read in Pelagius' commentary. These ideas.
do not appear in the extant material from Celestius, nor is
there any sure evidence that they formed part of that popu-
lar Pelagianism which gained ground in Carthage and'
Sicily.

Augustine in the two treatises from the period before 415
shows no inclination to be polemical directly against Pelagius. When his name is mentioned, it is in terms of high
respect, and Augustine explicitly wants to believe only the
best of him. One is justified, on the other hand, in seeing
evidence of veiled argument against him.

Much the same judgment must be made of Augustine's.
letters from the same period. The name of Pelagius appears in only one of them, that addressed to Pelagius himself.[52] The letter is short and amounts to an acknowledgment of a letter which Pelagius sent to Augustine giving the
bishop news "of his welfare." Augustine is brief, respectful,.

full of good wishes for his correspondent's spiritual well-being, and embarrassed by the eulogies which Pelagius in his letter has heaped upon him. It is most difficult to find in this letter any of the double meanings which Augustine will claim later that he had intended to insinuate.

One might be easily tempted to suppose that because the "Pelagian controversy" has "already begun," Augustine's letters in these years should betray an "overriding preoccupation" with it.[53] But the evidence for such preoccupation is scanty, the one important piece being the long letter 140. A certain Honoratus had written with questions on the proper exegesis of five scriptural texts, and Augustine took the occasion to organize part of his reply around the theme of the justifying grace of God and to warn against the enemies of grace who are unwilling to attribute their goodness to God.[54]

There is of course the important letter 157. This Augustine wrote in 414 to the Sicilian layman Hilarius directly in answer to a request for enlightenment on matters clearly related to the Pelagian controversy in the broad sense. But just as Augustine in his first treatise had concerned himself with points at issue among Christians at Carthage, so here his task is to deal with a number of theses being championed by certain Christians at Syracuse: (1) that sinlessness and keeping the commandments with ease are possible; (2) that unbaptized infants who die are not to be thought deprived of heaven; (3) that a rich man may enter the kingdom of heaven only if he divests himself of his riches; (4) that oath-taking is forbidden; (5) that the nature of the Church here and now is to be without spot or wrinkle.[55] The first and fourth of these are precise views of Pelagius.[56] They are views, however, which come to explicit expression in writings that Augustine has in 414 not read. The fifth, on the Church as without spot or wrinkle, does appear in Pelagius' commentary but not in prominent, developed form.[57] In any case Augustine's treatment of the fifth thesis amounts only to a short paragraph; by that point he wants to bring the letter quickly to a close and makes only the briefest comment on the Church as bearing along both good and bad to the end of the world.[58] With thesis (2) Pelagius would not have disagreed,[59] but there is no evidence that he ever taught thesis (3).[60]

We now know that Sicilian Pelagianism had its own theologian, a figure who was to be called "the Sicilian Briton." At least some of his writings we now possess. He was a man who had thoroughly read Pelagius' commentary on Paul and exploited it in his own writings. It is highly probable that he had met and talked at length with Pelagius on Sicily. But he carried Pelagian teaching to a degree of ascetic extremism which would have caused Pelagius no small dismay had he known of it.[61]

The fact and the character of Pelagius' relation to Sicilian Pelagianism is a subject about which Augustine would have known little.[62] The nearest he comes in letter 157 to a direct dealing with Pelagius is to recapitulate arguments from the work *On the Spirit and the Letter* on the law, on freedom of will, and on grace.[63] The fact important to remember is that Augustine is dealing with opinions disseminated among Christians in Sicily, and that Pelagius is far away in the Holy Land and has been there for some three years. Augustine could have been no more than curious as to whether Pelagius himself taught the five theses reported in Hilarius' letter.[64]

It is instructive to look at two sermons which Augustine preached at Carthage in 413, at an interval of three days apart. The first he preached on the Feast of the Nativity of St. John Baptist, and toward the end he included some remarks on original sin and on the baptism of infants. Children are to be baptized "lest they lose their heavenly inheritance"; when infants are brought to Jesus in baptism they are brought to no other end than the remission of sins; Christian people ought not to dispute this awesome matter lest they give the appearance of not caring about the salvation of infants.[65]

It would appear that no small tumult followed. The

preacher was accused certainly of innovation and probably of heresy as well.[66] The threat was noised about that those who taught the transmission of sin and the condemnation of unbaptized infants would be reported to the churches of the East and by them condemned.[67]

In the second sermon Augustine was to a degree conciliatory. He admitted that on such a subject a circumspect preacher ought to have said more than he had said and excused his brevity on the ground that the sermon had already gone on rather long.[68] To exhort his opponents as their friend was his intention, not to put them on trial as their enemy.[69] The preacher's shrewdness was revealed at that moment in the sermon when he read aloud from Cyprian; to the Carthaginian congregation he cited words in which the martyr bishop of their own city had justified the early baptism of infants on the ground that by their birth in the flesh they have contracted *contagium mortis antiquae*.[70]

Much of the sermon is given over to a discussion of the theory that infants are to be baptized not in order that they may attain salvation, i.e., eternal life, but in order that they may attain the higher state of the kingdom of heaven.[71] This is a theory that was clearly of importance in the Pelagianism of Carthage and may have been held by Celestius.[72] It is not a theory found anywhere in the writings of Pelagius, nor is it likely that he held it; he apparently made use of the distinction between eternal life and kingdom of heaven for the different purpose of specifying the disparate rewards awaiting married Christians and consecrated virgins respectively.[73] Toward the end of his sermon Augustine shows that he has not forgotten what he has read in Pelagius' commentary. He takes up his own rather specialized interpretation of two of the arguments against original sin.[74] Pelagius had recorded the opinion that the offspring of baptized parents could scarcely inherit what their parents no longer possess, i.e., original sin. Augustine now makes this argument equal to the absurd suggestion that the children of baptized parents should by their birth already be in possession of the righteousness of Christ, adding the rhetorical question, "Would you have it that a son of a baptized father be born already baptized, although you see that a son of a circumcised father is not born already circumcised?" [75] Another of the arguments had contended that if the sin of Adam injures those who themselves have not sinned, then Christ must be of benefit to those who have not believed. Augustine agrees with the implication of the argument. It is absurd to suggest that Christ can be of benefit apart from faith. He then confines the application of the phrase "those who have not believed," to infants at baptism (thus undoubtedly reducing the full force of the argument), and offers his solution that infants may be thought to believe by the faith of their parents. And if they are cleansed by the faith of parents, we may without difficulty presume them to have been defiled by the sin of parents.[76]

In his closing remarks Augustine announces, regarding the opinions he has been opposing, that although he could perhaps call people heretics who hold such views, he nonetheless does not call them such.[77] They are to be held within the bosom of their mother the Church in the hope that they may be healed and taught. The mistaken disputers are to be borne in patience; they have gone astray in matters which they have not examined with sufficient care and which they have not allowed to be determined by the mature authority of the Church.[78]

Let us summarize the results of our survey so far. Before the writing of his treatise *On Nature and Grace* in 415 Augustine has been engaged in a Pelagian controversy in three respects: (1) he has written against views held by Christians in Carthage and in Sicily; (2) he has opposed arguments on the subject of original sin found in Pelagius' commentary but which he expressly refuses to believe are opinions of Pelagius; (3) in a relatively irenical treatise he has probably had in mind Pelagius' commentary when arguing against views on free will, divine assistance as law, and the nature of that law by which no man is justified. Augustine has been chiefly called upon so far to deal with problems in Africa and Sicily. He has no particular reason to identify Pelagius with the Sicilian theses as a whole, nor does he do so. Of Pelagius' brief stay in Africa he expressly writes that after the man had been at Hippo in the bishop's absence, his own subsequent inquiry was able to produce no evidence that Pelagius while there had disputed against the grace of God.[79]

Let us now for a moment jump over the year 415 and look back with Augustine from the year 417. He gives us two rather different views of his private and written opinion concerning Pelagius in the period before he wrote the work *On Nature and Grace*. Each of these views contains a large measure of credibility, yet each fails finally to convince on the terms in which Augustine states it. On the one hand, he clearly suggests that as early as 412 he thought that Pelagius held erroneous views on the subject of grace. He is upset by the way in which Pelagius at the Synod of Diospolis produced in his support the letter which Augustine had sent to him in 412. The letter, we recall, was a courteous and cordial note. In his survey and commentary on the proceedings of the synod, Augustine claims that the note had really contained a veiled admonition that Pelagius should come to a proper knowledge of the grace of God.[80] The claim does not quite carry conviction. On a dispassionate reading it is most difficult to discover in the letter the current of meaning which its author now wishes to infuse into it. But Augustine is now undoubtedly revealing something of his state of mind about Pelagius at the time when he wrote the cordial note. He already had some cause for alarm, from oral report and from his reading of the Pauline commentary.[81]

On the other hand, in a letter to Paulinus of Nola, also from 417, he writes that it was Pelagius' book *On Nature* which persuaded him that its author had the intention of destroying in the hearts of the faithful any belief in grace bestowed upon men through Jesus Christ.[82] Before reading this book, Augustine writes, "we loved him as one who seemed to be of the true faith." [83] In this second account, then, it is the work *On Nature* which by a sudden shock awakened him to the danger posed by Pelagius' teaching on grace.

Common to both of those accounts is Augustine's recalling he had had it by oral report that Pelagius was opposing the grace of God, and he now has a correspondingly dual memory of what he had made of this rumor. In the first account he seems clearly to suggest that on the basis of this oral report he believed the man to be an opponent of grace and thus inserted the veiled insinuations into his letter to Pelagius. In fact he writes that the report which had reached him was causing him much pain, in that "it was recounted to me by people whom I trusted." [84] In his letter to Pelagius' old friend Paulinus, on the other hand, Augustine assures his correspondent that he had not believed the rumor, "for rumor is usually a liar." [85]

If the first of the above accounts does not quite convince, neither does the second. We have seen reason to believe that in the work *On the Spirit and the Letter,* Augustine took issue with views on grace, law, and freedom which he would have read in Pelagius' Pauline commentary. We know that by the time of writing *On the Spirit and the Letter* Augustine had already read the commentary; he informs us of this himself.[86] Although it is true, as is often said, that the treatise *On the Spirit and the Letter* is relatively speaking an irenic one, its author is nonetheless opposing doctrines which he believes to be false. A proponent of such views he would scarcely have wanted to describe as "seeming to be of the true faith." Further, Augustine's letter to Paulinus requires us to believe that Pelagius' work *On Nature* presented something crucial and new, forcing the decision that its author was propagating "evil views by which the coming of the Savior is made void." [87] Nor is it only from the letter to Paulinus that we know of Augustine's view of the work *On Nature* as the turning point in his attitude toward Pelagius. In his book *On the Proceedings of Pelagius,* Augustine recalls his initial uncertainty over the teachings of Pelagius and how it was in his reading of the work *On Nature* that "it became very evident to me—too evident, indeed, to admit of any further doubt—how hostile to salvation by Christ was his poisonous perversion of the truth." [88] And it was this book which Augustine and four other bishops sent to Innocent, with certain passages marked for special attention, as part of the African enterprise to stir the papacy to action against Pelagius and Celestius.[89]

We thus come to a critical question: What was it in the work *On Nature* which so convinced Augustine that Pelagius was a man to fight? The question requires two answers, one negative and one positive. The negative answer is quite simply that in the work *On Nature* there appears to be no theological teaching *to which Augustine seriously objects* which was not also present in Pelagius' commentary on Paul. It is of course regrettable that such first-hand knowledge as we have of the work *On Nature* comes from the fragments with which Augustine supplies us in his work *On Nature and Grace*. But this very circumstance would lead us naturally to suppose that the passages of greatest offense would be among the ones which Augustine would choose to quote and upon which he would comment. One may readily admit that Pelagius' treatise was presumably a piece of extended prose writing, whereas the commentary consists for the most part in rather short notes on single verses and parts of verses. But erroneous teaching can be communicated clearly enough in exegetical comments of the length of those found in Pelagius' earlier work. A solution to the problem is not to be found by contrasting the types of writing to be found in the two works of Pelagius.

It would appear from Augustine's treatise that a considerable part of Pelagius' book was given over to a discussion of related subjects centering on the problem of original sin. We find the following positions of Pelagius: an infant dying unbaptized is not condemned;[90] if a man were of such a character that he could not possibly be without sin, he would be free of blame;[91] our human nature has been neither crippled nor transformed by sin because sin is not a "substance";[92] sin is *perperam facti actus;*[93] the commission of more sins cannot be thought to be punishment for sin;[94] no evil may be the cause of any good, and therefore it is absurd to posit sin as the cause of God's mercy or as the necessary precondition of there being no sin;[95] there is no sin that is not pride, and there is no guilt from a sin that is not one's own voluntary sin;[96] we are said to sin "in Adam" because of our imitation of Adam's sin.[97] Not all of these particular assertions find precise counterparts in Pelagius' commentary, and it is clear that Pelagius in the later work is shoring up his position with some new arguments. But it is equally clear that the central issue for both Pelagius and Augustine, so far as this series of assertions goes, is that of a doctrine of sin and guilt as transmitted by procreation to all the children of Adam. It is worth recalling here that in the eyes of the later Augustine the denial of original sin is one of the three chief points of Pelagian heresy.[98] In a letter from the year 418, Augustine could write that Pelagius and Celestius are judged to be the "most manifest heretics" because of their denial of the transmission of sin from Adam to infants.[99] One could not suppose from reading the commentary on Paul that Pelagius when composing that work had been patient of a doctrine of original sin.

It might be argued that whereas Pelagius had not explicitly assumed responsibility himself for the famous four arguments against original sin, he now openly acknowledges his opposition. But it is doubtful that Augustine or anyone reading the commentary could take seriously the notion that Pelagius disapproved or was neutral in respect of these arguments. When Pelagius inserts comments that take up as much space as these arguments require, he is talking about something about which he cares. From places in the commentary, moreover, where Pelagius gives no suggestion of writing in the name of persons other than himself, it is evident that he has no doctrine of original sin and that he believes Adam to have injured men by offering an example of sin which they have imitated.[100] This doctrine of sin by the imitation of Adam is stated clearly in the commentary and yet it does not evoke Augustine's written opposition to Pelagius until he reads it in the work *On Nature*.

The same thesis holds true about other important assertions and points of exegesis against which Augustine sets himself in the work *On Nature and Grace,* having become acquainted with them when he read Pelagius' commentary three years before.[101]

There is one significant item of teaching in the work *On Nature* which does not appear in the commentary, at least does not appear in the same formulation. Sensing himself under pressure to say whether man is able to avoid sin without the help of grace, Pelagius now defines the capacity to avoid sin, implanted in man by the Creator, as a gift of grace.[102] Augustine takes exception to a number of definitions and analogies by which Pelagius approaches his statement of this doctrine.[103] But to the doctrine itself, understood as applying to the original state of man at creation, Augustine does not object. He could not very well have objected, as he himself had a parallel though not identical doctrine.[104] The bishop insists only that the point at issue is not that grace by which man is made but, rather, that grace by which man is remade in Jesus Christ. Since Pelagius himself has raised the question of grace, argues Augustine, and since he is silent concerning the grace by which we are saved, we are allowed to conclude that he holds such grace to be unnecessary.[105] A like argument could be applied to the commentary, where it is not Pelagius but the Apostle Paul who raises the issue of grace through Jesus Christ. Pelagius in the commentary does indeed give expression to a doctrine of grace as forgiveness of sins through the death of Jesus Christ.[106] But grace understood as forgiveness is not enough for Augustine,[107] and the Pelagius of the commentary does not have a doctrine which Augustine could recognize as positing that grace by which human nature is remade.

Augustine's decisive reaction against Pelagius' work *On Nature* cannot be adequately explained by any new teaching which he found there, not having been acquainted with it before as a teaching of Pelagius. We come then to the second and positive answer to our large question: Augustine reacts decisively to the work *On Nature* because he finds there a whole section in which Pelagius has supported his own position by quoting from works of weighty Catholic authors: Lactantius, Hilary of Poitiers, Ambrose, John Chrysostom, Xystus the Martyr bishop of Rome, Jerome, and finally Augustine himself.[108] Pelagius becomes a serious threat at that moment when Augustine sees him marshaling the forces of Catholic orthodoxy behind him. Of one thing Augustine was certain—that on the important doctrines of sin, grace, and freedom he spoke with no other voice than that of the Catholic Church.

It would be wide of the mark to form a picture of Pelagius the proud innovator, unlearned in Christian theology, sitting down to work at his book *On Nature* and hectically extracting isolated passages from Catholic authors hurriedly read. From the earliest period of his literary activity, he had widely studied the works of respected authors, as the researches of Smith and Bohlin have demonstrated.[109] He had not followed any of them slavishly but had selected both ideas and precise language for the formation of a theology markedly anti-Manichaean in its direction. In particular he had studied the earliest of Augustine's anti-Manichaean works, *On Free Choice*, and quoted this work in his own book *On Nature*. He had found material there of importance for his own thought, such as the distinction between "nature" and "necessity," on the one hand, and "will," on the other; the freedom of individual men to turn to the good; the confining power of sin as the power of "habit"; and sin as "ignorance" of the divine will.[110]

Augustine became highly sensitive to the Pelagian use of his own treatise and was able with some justice to point to passages in it where "long before the Pelagian heresy arose, we debated as though we were already debating against them." [111] But the dialogue in three books *On Free Choice* is a work that is at unity neither with itself nor with the later and more developed theology of its author. He began it only two years after his conversion to Catholic Christian faith and finished it over a period of six or seven years, years interspersed with a renewed study of Paul's epistle to the Romans.[112] Within its pages, for example, we see Augustine having arrived at a halfway house on the way toward his full doctrine of original sin: as punishment for the sin of Adam the children of men are visited with a dual condition—ignorance of the divine will and a moral constriction such that they are unable to do such good as they know and will to do; this dual condition and such acts as flow inevitably from it are denoted by the term "sin," although, significantly, neither the condition nor the acts bring guilt upon the individual; guilt is counted only when the soul does not seek to replace its ignorance with knowledge and put itself in the way of moral "power" when the opportunity for these advantages occurs.[113] This is obviously far from the doctrine of original sin which Augustine was later to formulate and to insist upon as traditional Catholic teaching.

On two further matters Augustine in 413–415 shows that he has either forgotten or abandoned positions which he had taken in his earliest anti-Manichaean work, and these are matters which bear directly upon his polemic against Pelagius. In his book *On Nature*, Pelagius makes a point of fundamental importance to his argument against the inevitability of sin: "Whatever is bound by natural necessity is thereby lacking in the choice and deliberation proper to will." [114] The statement is indicative of Pelagius' enduring anti-Manichaean stance and is reminiscent of a number of passages in his other works.[115] Augustine in 415 quibbles at Pelagius' distinction between will and natural necessity, arguing that men's desire to be happy is both matter of will and matter of necessity.[116] But it was Augustine himself who had made Pelagius' precise point with great elaboration in the third book of his work *On Free Choice*. A stone thrown up into the air falls to the ground by necessity of nature, whereas when the soul moves from enjoyment of the Creator to enjoyment of the creature, it does so by a movement of its own will, a movement unlike that of the stone.[117] Augustine's refusal to see Pelagius' point in 415 exemplifies not only his failure to penetrate to the heart of his opponent's position but also his blotting out of his own theological past.

Then there is the matter of will understood as a "middle good." In the second book of the work *On Free Choice*, Augustine had employed a distinction among three kinds of "goods": "great goods," to which the virtues belong; "minimal goods," to which various kinds of bodily beauty belong, and "middle goods," to which will belongs.[118] The great goods are by definition not susceptible of being used wrongly, but the middle and minimal goods are susceptible of being used both rightly and wrongly.[119] Having made these distinctions, Augustine goes on to elaborate the theme of free will as belonging to those things which we use either for good or for ill, suggesting that will can be thought to possess a kind of self-transcendence and thus to "use" itself, just as reason itself is one of the things which reason knows and memory itself is remembered through memory.[120] Now although Pelagius never avails himself of this precise way of speaking about will, it is clear that Augustine's conception here is entirely congruent with Pelagius' repeated insistence that man's freedom of choice is a freedom for both good and evil.[121]

In his first anti-Pelagian treatise, Augustine is of a different mind on this subject. Without explicitly recalling his earlier position, he now makes two points of fundamental importance for his developing understanding of will. (1) If will is a kind of instrument which we may use for either good or ill, and if it is God who gives this will but we who make it a good will, "then that which comes from ourselves is better than that which comes from him," and we are unable to say with the Apostle, "What hast thou that thou didst not receive?" (2) Will would be "an extraordinary

thing" if it could exist *in medio* as neither good nor evil.
Will is either good or evil, according as we either do or do
not love righteousness. A good will, then, is a gift from
God and it belongs to that class of goods which it is impossible to misuse.[122] What we observe here is an instance of
Augustine's shift away from an image of man as autonomous
chooser among moral possibilities to an image of man as
inescapably turned either toward or away from God and as
turned toward God only through the power of the divine
grace. The first image was relevant to his anti-Manichaean
polemic. It is one of Augustine's weaknesses as a theologian
that these images are never satisfactorily related to each
other.

The tension between the two was already present in the
six or seven years through which he was composing his
books *On Free Choice*. The problem of the internal consistency of the work can be illustrated by the following:
in Book I the author can write in neo-Platonic vein,
". . . Whoever wishes to live rightly and virtuously, if he
wishes so to wish in preference to the goods that are but
passing, acquires this great possession with such ease, that
to wish for it is the same as to possess what he wished";[123]
in Book III he writes, "When we speak of a will free to act
rightly, we speak of the will with which man was created,"[124]
and contrasts this will with that hemmed in by ignorance
and impotence which are the results of fallen man's condemnation. Augustine's retrospective attempt to view the
books *On Free Choice* as written throughout from a unitary
perspective simply fails to convince.

In fact Augustine's early work *On Free Choice* offers
within its own covers a microcosm of that vast world of uncertainty and of clashing views in patristic writings East
and West and up into the fifth century, on man fallen and
unfallen, on sin, and on grace. Pelagius was able to take
widely scattered elements from this confused picture and
press them into easy service for a theology that is at once
Western, legal, and moralistic, and at the same time draws

sustenance from Eastern perspectives on creation and human freedom.

The course of the controversy over Pelagius turns upon the appeal to authority. In reading the book *On Nature* Augustine saw in Pelagius a figure whom he could no longer continue to treat with distant respect as a celebrated holy man, while politely overlooking theological disagreements. Pelagius was now making an explicit claim upon the history of Christian theology, a history which extended up into the early Augustine himself. The issue in 415 between Pelagius and Augustine could be formulated broadly as follows: Which theological synthesis, which attempt to bring clarity, which novelty will prevail?

Chapter 6

——◆——

THE THEOLOGY OF PELAGIUS

THE PRESENT essay is intended to be expository in a limited sense. The attempt will be to present a balanced summary of Pelagius' teaching, and to do this allowing his own emphases to establish the lines of exposition. But immediately it must be said that the project here is not to present a complete mosaic in which every subject to which Pelagius gives attention would find its place, but rather to delineate his theology as it centers on the fundamental problem of man and the saving activity of God in which man participates. Critical questions as to the literary, theological, and philosophical sources of his thought will here be largely suppressed; hopefully this chapter, in attempting to establish the content of Pelagius' teaching, will be of assistance toward further research into such sources.[1] There can be no exposition without interpretation; I hope that references will be given sufficiently to make the line clear between interpretative comment and Pelagius' explicit statement.

If excuse is needed for presenting at this time a summary statement of Pelagius' thought, it may be said that recent individual expositions of Pelagius differ from that to be offered here in one or more of three basic respects: in abstracting Pelagius' teaching on grace and freedom from its broader context;[2] in assuming a list of Pelagius' extant writings which is either too long,[3] or too short;[4] in being less clearly theological in interest and method.[5]

Before proceeding further it may be well to clarify one more point. We should today possibly not be mindful of the figure of Pelagius were it not for the controversy over grace and freedom which takes its name from him. Probably most theological interest in Pelagius is generated at least from an initial interest in that controversy. This is admittedly the case in the present chapter. From an initial interest in the Pelagian controversy, I shall attempt to summarize the thought of Pelagius in such a way as to allow his teaching on freedom and grace to stand exposed as part of a larger theological scheme. Thus to state my intention is immediately to raise two further problems. First, the question may be asked: Does Pelagius' teaching on freedom and grace have for his larger theological scheme a like importance to that which it had for the controversy surrounding his name? The answer to this question cannot be a simple Yes or No, and a properly ambiguous answer will be given in due course. Second, the question may be asked: Does Pelagius really give expression to a rounded theology of a sort that is possible to recover? Pelagius does at least give expression to a more complete theological scheme than would be supposed if one were simply to contrast his assertions on grace and freedom with parallel assertions from St. Augustine, or if one were to take his controversial assertions on grace and freedom as themselves constituting his theological scheme. To present a sympathetic and balanced account of this larger scheme, and thus to assist in making intelligible the theological position of one of the central figures in the controversy—this is the present task. It is common to say that Pelagius was a moralist and not much of a theologian. There is perhaps this much truth to the commonplace: Pelagius was a clearer and more explicit moralist than theologian in the proper sense, and both his writings and activity display a preoccupation with the concrete problems of the Christian life. But theologian he was also, and to his theology we now turn.

The thought of Pelagius as a whole is governed by three

principal motifs. He wishes first to be an orthodox theologian of the Catholic Church and to be known as such. His early writing[6] on the Trinity makes it clear that he is tolerant of no doctrine of God save a Trinitarian one which upholds the unity of substance and distinguishes the persons. We have fragments[7] from what appears to have been a treatise on Christology in which Pelagius is seen particularly as an opponent of Apollinarianism. The commentary on Paul is generously sprinkled with polemical references and arguments against Arians, Macedonians, Photinians, Apollinarians, Novatians, Marcionites, and Jovinianists.[8] It is clear that as a theological writer Pelagius has no intention other than to think in and with the Catholic Church.

Second, Pelagius' theology finds its center of gravity in the problem of man—his nature, his relation to God, and his moral obligation. This is not to say that anthropology is the whole of Pelagius' theology. It is to say, rather, that if one is to find a central and organizing principle by which the largest number of his single teachings may be related to each other, that principle is his fundamental conception of the nature and obligation of man.

The third motif is closely related to the second. Pelagius wishes to formulate his conception of man in such a way as to make the Christian doctrine of man clearly distinguishable from Manichaean notions of man and so as to combat whatever influences and traces of Manichaeism are to be found within the Church.[9]

MAN AS RATIONAL CREATURE

To speak of man means immediately to speak of him as a creature of God. The whole dignity of man lies precisely in his being a peculiar, special creature of God. To measure human moral possibilities requires that we consider the Creator of man, since man among the creatures has a peculiar relation and likeness to God. This peculiar relation Pelagius specifies by the related ideas of reason, law of nature, conscience, and natural goodness. By his endowment with reason man is able to use the nonhuman creation for his own ends and to defend himself from its ravages. By this same endowment man as originally created is able to acknowledge God as Lord of creation and to know himself as servant of God. This natural acknowledgment of the Creator means concretely the ability to know the will of God for man, the ability to distinguish the morally good from the morally base and the awareness that man is summoned by the Creator to perform the former. The activity of reason includes the natural awareness of the law of nature which is written on the heart, a law which does not deceive but which directs man reliably to action in conformity to his own nature, which in turn is action in conformity to the will of God. The law of nature then is given by reason applying itself to the concrete business of moral choice between good and evil; awareness of the law of nature is virtually identical with conscience, the interior judge which presides in the soul as moral teacher, approving praiseworthy acts and disapproving base ones. "Natural goodness" is the term which denotes the rational creature's capacity both to act in accord with the law of nature and to reject that law. Man's natural goodness means voluntary goodness, the chief glory of the rational soul being its capacity for good that is spontaneously willed. By implanting within man the "capacity for either direction" [10] God himself has brought it about that what man wills is the fruit of his own autonomous choice. Such autonomous choice is the condition of any meaningful talk about human virtue.[11]

As over against the nonhuman creation man's natural goodness is clarified as will, which is contrasted to natural necessity.[12] Our extant material from Pelagius does not give us as much help as we might like in understanding the precise way in which Pelagius conceives this contrast, but he very likely had in mind a passage from Augustine's work *On Free Choice,* a work which he quoted in his own defense, as was noted above in Chapter 5. There Augustine makes the point that a stone thrown into the air returns to the ground "by necessity of nature," a movement contrasted to that of the soul which moves from enjoyment of the Creator to enjoyment of the creature. The movement of the soul is unlike that of the stone in that it is a movement which the soul itself determines, a movement of will.[13]

Man as a creature endowed with will therefore does not sin by a necessity imposed upon the will from without. Nor can the promptings of man's own flesh be thought to impose a "necessity of sinning." When man sins he turns away from the law of his own nature and in so doing turns away from the will of God, and this bending of the will away from the law of nature is always a bending of *will*, i.e., is not an inevitable result of conditions exterior to will.[14] And Pelagius can also employ the distinction between will and necessity in another direction. Man is not "bound to the necessity of unchanging goodness";[15] there is no necessity issuing from the divine will which compels men to obey. Will is irreducibly characterized by its own freedom of choice as it is related both to the will of God and to the non-human creation.

Man's place as a created rational being in the context of the natural order leads Pelagius to a twofold use of the concept "nature." On the one hand, man as possessing rational will is set off against "nature," which is the realm of necessity. On the other hand, man possesses his own "nature" which is characterized by freedom of choice either to act in accord with its own law or not. Nature in this second sense is possessed of its own peculiar kind of "necessity": it is of the "necessity" of man's nature that he possess freedom of choice. By speaking thus Pelagius wishes to be emphatic in making his point that man's "capacity for either direction" is itself nothing for which man may take credit but is wholly due to the creative activity of God; that man possesses freedom of choice is not itself due to his exercise of that freedom.[16]

We are brought thus to one facet of Pelagius' doctrine of

grace. Man's "capacity for either direction" means in fact
that man is able to be without sin. This genuine possibility
of sinlessness, defined as a divinely implanted "natural"
capacity, Pelagius designates as unintelligible except as bestowed by the grace of God. Whether he ever would have
expressed this precise idea apart from the pressure of controversy is a moot point. The fact is that we discover him
saying this only in the fragments from his two works written
in the heat of controversy, when he must answer the question whether he teaches that men may achieve sinlessness
without the grace of God. The answer which he returns is
that the capacity (*posse*) to be without sin pertains in the
first instance properly to God, who bestows it upon his
creature.[17] This bestowal of a divine property cannot then
be interpreted except by the notion of "grace." Alternately
he can explain himself as meaning that the capacity in question is a matter of the necessity of man's nature and that
what pertains to such necessity has been placed there by
God, the Author of nature, and is therefore to be called
"grace." [18] Thus it is not clear whether Pelagius means to
say that the capacity for sinlessness is a gift of grace (1) because such a capacity results from the bestowing upon man
of an attribute belonging properly and in the first instance
to God, or (2) because such a capacity, belonging to the
necessity of man's nature, can only have been implanted
there by the Creator of man's nature.

It could be argued that he means (2) rather than (1) because of the absurdity on Pelagius' own grounds of taking
(1) seriously: man's capacity is characteristically in Pelagius
"the capacity for either direction," [19] and if this capacity
results from the bestowing upon man of a like divine capacity, we are involved in speaking of the divine capacity for
sin. But so to interpret would involve us in an outright re-
jection of (1), on the ground that muddleheaded Pelagius
could not possibly have been aware of what he was saying.

A better interpretation, which will not entirely acquit
Pelagius of confusion in language, is to take (2) as the clue

to the meaning of (1) and to interpret both in the light of
the ambiguity of meaning attaching to "necessity," as follows: it pertains to the necessity of *man's* nature that he be
free of external necessity; freedom from external necessity
is in the first instance a property of the nature of God and
is derivatively God's gift to man; thus that *posse,* which in
the case of God would mean his freedom over against all
that is not God, means when bestowed upon man the
capacity to be without sin.[20]

However problematic Pelagius' explicit arguments may
remain, two things at least are clear: (1) Pelagius wants us
to understand as gift of grace man's unique status as set
over against the necessities of nature and as possessing the
capacity for spontaneously willed sinlessness. (2) Man's possession of this gift offers him no opportunity for boasting;
it appears that the real significance of associating the capacity with the term "grace" is to remove any possible suggestion that man may take credit for possessing it.[21]

THE TIMES OF NATURE AND OF LAW

Pelagius sees the history of the race as a history in three
stages with two great turning points. He speaks specifically
of the three "times": the time of nature, extending from
Adam to Moses; the time of the law, extending from Moses
to Christ; and the time of grace, inaugurated by Christ.[22]
Moses and Christ are the two pivotal figures.[23] The fact that
the three times are designated in this way and that Moses
and Christ are the two key figures offers an important clue
to Pelagius' understanding both of man's history and of
God's dealings with man. The first period, as the period of
nature, is one in which man's original created nature is
still, at least in some men, visible and operative. The second
and third periods are those in which God acts, first through
Moses and then in Christ, to restore that nature to its
original state. Creation, then, and two stages in which that
creation is repaired, offer the basic framework within which
Pelagius sees man and his history.

There is a sense in which Adam too is a pivotal figure, although he is this in a less important sense than Moses and Christ. History really turns upon the creative and restorative acts of God, and Adam as first sinner thus cannot occupy the determinative roles of the other two figures. Pelagius is indeed perfectly clear that Adam was in fact the first sinner. Nor does he hesitate to agree with the words of the Apostle Paul that sin entered the world through the one man Adam. By this he means simply that men allowed themselves to follow the example set by Adam in disobeying the will of God.[24] The injury which Adam worked upon his descendants was the injury of being both the first man and the first disobedient man, and this injury takes its effect through man's fateful living by the model of that disobedience.

It is well known that Pelagius is not tolerant of any doctrine of original sin understood as the transmission of sin through procreation. The arguments in his writings which militate against such a doctrine are surveyed elsewhere in this book.[25] The heart of the matter seems to lie in two central considerations: the fundamental definition of sin and the determination not to yield to any teaching which smacks of Manichaean determinism and dualism. On the one hand, sin is act, the act of an individual; it is "the performance of a deed wrongly done." [26] No man can be said to be guilty except for a deed which proceeds from his own individual will.[27] On the other hand, to speak of sin by transmission is to take the discussion of sin out of the only context in which it makes sense on Christian terms; it is to make sin a *necessary* component of human existence and thus to fall into Manichaeism. To make sin necessary would be to deny the nature of will, whose only necessity lies in its capacity both to sin and not to sin.[28] Likewise would a doctrine of transmitted sin seem to involve a view of sin as active in such a way as to cripple and transform man's created nature; this crippling and transforming power would only be possible if there were a "substance" which had been created as an evil component of man's nature, which again he sees as the equivalent of Manichaean doctrine.[29] To these two principal considerations is to be added the creationist doctrine of the soul, which Pelagius assumed; to combine the creationist doctrine with a view of sin as transmitted would be inevitably to conceive sin as afflicting the body only and not the soul, which is nonsense.[30] These various points may all be drawn together by a more general observation: Pelagius makes it perfectly and explicitly clear that in his mind the birth of a child is tied directly to the doctrine of creation; that which is in man at birth is that which God has created, and God is the Author only of that which is good.[31] Pelagius does, however, have a doctrine of the power of sin not viewed as derived from the relation of men to Adam as progeny to progenitor. This will receive attention in a more appropriate place.

The period of time from Adam to Moses is the "time of nature." The chief thing which Pelagius wishes to say about this phase of human history is that it offers us examples of men who did in fact live in accord with the law of nature and were thus successful in leading sinless lives.[32] The condemnation of death in punishment for sin was not visited upon all men in this period, but upon those (the vast majority) who despised the law of their own being and fell into sin.[33] Whereas Adam had been warned by a precise and explicitly given commandment of God, these other men were equipped only with their own nature, which was sufficient to them as law and which preserved them without sin in accord with their own free choice.[34] Such were Abel, Noah, Melchizedek, Abraham, and Job, among others. These were "Gospel men before the Gospel," "disciples of the apostles." They display the riches which lie untapped within all of us who are now unaware of what our human nature is capable.[35]

These ancient sinless men followed the law of nature but in doing so were out of step with the vast multitudes even of their own time.[36] In fact the time came when human nature was no longer sufficient to men as law. It was no longer sufficient, not because that nature underwent a transformation, but because men became oblivious of it. Moral corruption brought it about that man's reason was enveloped in darkness. It became overlaid with a coating of rust, the rust of ignorance. Human history then entered its second phase. Through the agency of Moses God gave to men the law.[37]

Pelagius conceives the law of Moses chiefly as the means provided by God by which to remedy the condition of man's ignorance as to his own nature. The law was to be a file. By constant application of its abrasive injunctions the rust of ignorance was to be done away and man's newly polished nature was to stand out again in its pristine brilliance.[38] It is clear that Pelagius attributes chief significance to the "moral" aspects of the law of Moses and that he gives only a temporary and secondary value to its ceremonial requirements.[39] The feast days of the Jews had their historical appropriateness as aids in preserving them from idolatry;[40] circumcision is given a variety of justifications, among which that thus the people of God could be known among the Gentiles, that their bodies could be recognized in war, and that it was a sign of the special worth which in the time of grace would be given to chastity.[41] Pelagius admits in effect that he as a Christian is looking back retrospectively upon the law of Moses and that the law cannot be properly understood until its *finis* has appeared, until Christ is believed.[42] It is the gospel in fact which has given us moral and ethical laws, as opposed to the old ordinances of circumcision and the like.[43]

There are three further important points to be made about the law and the "time of the Law." First, the law of Moses did in fact open up again the possibility that men would obey the will of God and thus attain eternal life, and Pelagius is willing even to mention names of those who were able to live without sin in the "time of the Law." [44] Second, God in his justice did not lay upon the Jews any moral requirements which were impossible of fulfilling. Pelagius adopts a very simple exegesis of the Apostle's thesis that the law did not justify: it did not justify because in fact the generality of God's people did not keep it but rather despised it.[45] Third, the law is properly to be described as "grace," and Pelagius is quick to seize the opportunity to be polemical against any such as Manichaeans and Marcionites who deprecate this means by which was opened to man the possibility of rediscovering both the law of his own nature and the will of God.[46]

THE TIME OF GRACE

The Problem of Sin

It is the view of Pelagius that by the time human history reached that point at which the time of grace begins, the generality of men were held by a power of sin so strong that not even the law of Moses was able to free them from it. This remains the precise condition of men except as they come under the liberating sway of Christ. It is also the view of Pelagius that all men without exception are able to be without sin. Are these two propositions involved in hopeless contradiction, are we to interpret them as "paradoxical" or "dialectical," or is it simply a matter of the definition of terms? For purposes of expounding Pelagius, it is better, at least at first, to avoid notions of paradox and dialectic and to attend to what he says. Not every problem will thereby be solved, and it will be necessary to fill in one or two gaps.

The power which sin holds over men is the power of habit, a power which builds itself up through successive acts of sinning.[47] The ideas of "habit" and of "example" in Pelagius are to be interpreted as correlative. Men learn to sin by their existence from childhood alongside others who sin. They are swept along the wide road which leads to destruction in company with the vast multitude of men who are oblivious of the law of their own nature. Habit infects us from childhood and gradually corrupts us more and more through many years.[48] Pelagius can even write that habit holds the sinner "as if by a certain necessity of sinning,"[49] but it is a necessity which he has prepared for himself,[50] i.e., not one that is imposed upon him by the fact of his birth or by the mere constituents of which he is made. Sinful habit is productive of a condition of ignorance; our reason is lost in a cloud; the law of nature is in oblivion, buried.[51]

For this situation the idea of "law" plays an interesting and complex role. On the one hand, Pelagius retains his conviction that that which liberates the law of man's nature is law which comes from God. "Law" answers to "law." The law of God in Scripture is a mirror in which the soul may perceive its own image.[52] Only law from God is able to overcome the power of habitual sin.[53] Yet the law of Moses is no longer able to do this because of the excessive power of habit,[54] and man under that law must await a more powerful law. The law of Moses can at this stage only stir the sense of guilt and make man aware that sin is sin.[55] That it does, but it does not penetrate the obstructive layers with which habit has buried man's natural goodness.[56] Apart from the coming of Christ man senses the law as imposed from some alien source rather than as corresponding to his own rational nature.[57] For man bound by the power of sinful habit who in this condition now hears the law, the effect which it has upon him is to make him aware of his transgression.[58] Or to use another metaphor, which Pelagius takes from Scripture and Christian tradition, the "wide way" leading to destruction is the more appealing because of its superficially pleasant delights, whereas the "narrow way" to life appears disagreeable, leading over unapproachable heights. This is the situation until we shall have reached that condition of unobstructed awareness of our own now hidden nature, a condition in which conscience can again bear its natural witness, and we shall have discovered that the paths of righteousness may be walked with ease.[59] Apart from Christ men in the time of grace are therefore seen as standing in a twofold condition: they are guilty before God for the sins which they have committed,[60] and they are powerless to overcome the habit of sinning.[61]

Pelagius describes this situation of man as one in which he is in a certain way duplex and divided within himself.[62] Such tension he can but does not often express as a tension between soul and body in this sense: the rational soul gives its assent to the law of God, whereas the tendency of body is to suggest to man that he should pursue physical pleasures which are repugnant to reason; if these promptings gain the ascendancy, as they have, man is thereby subjected to the "law of sin," so that soul, or conscience, or the "divine law in the mind," cannot effectively assert itself.[63] It is surely no accident that Pelagius seldom employs the contrast soul-body or soul-flesh in expressing this tension. He wishes to avoid the idea that flesh or body is a "contrary substance" to soul or spirit, which he understands as Manichaean doctrine. His insistence is that God has not joined flesh to spirit to the end that there be a "necessity of sinning." [64] But whether he employs the contrast soul-body or his preferred contrasts of knowledge-ignorance, law of nature-habit of sinning, his teaching is clear that in the "time of grace" the generality of men are without power to overcome the effect of sinful habit.[65]

Nonetheless man is able to be without sin. An intelligible meaning is not difficult to assign to this assertion if the exposition so far has been correct and further if attention is paid to the contexts within which Pelagius most clearly makes the assertion. By way of underlining what has been said so far, we may note Pelagius' use of the revealing image of the soul as a treasure vault containing the hidden riches of man's nature. The soul's treasure is one "which we possess without using it." [66] Chief among the riches of human nature of course is the capacity to live in accord with the law of nature and thus to be without sin. This capacity is one which endures even though it remain untapped. For Pelagius to say that men "are able" to be without sin, therefore, means that they possess a resource which their present condition places beyond their grasp. To admit that man is not able to be without sin would be to undercut the total structure of language which Pelagius has built in speaking of man. It would be to admit that man has become something other than man, and this Pelagius refuses to do. Man is still that creature whom God created as man; the doctrine of creation remains determinative. If the question be posed as to why the treasure remains untapped, then the answer lies ready to hand that the effect of habitual sinning has been such as to eradicate from men's consciousness the empowering awareness of their own nature. The close interrelatedness of the terms "reason," "conscience," "law of nature," and "capacity for sinlessness," on the one hand, and the like interrelatedness of "habit," "oblivion," "ignorance," and "a kind of necessity of sinning," on the other, are of obvious importance for an understanding of Pelagius' language. From one point of view man is always "able" to be without sin; from another point of view even the present will to be without sin, spurred by knowledge of the old law, is without its effect.[67] We may put the point this way: It lies beyond the grasp of man to know and to be what he is and remains.

But one may also learn something from a consideration of the contexts in which Pelagius makes statements about the enduring possibility of sinlessness. These occur chiefly in his two argumentative treatises and in the statement of faith which he sent to Pope Innocent, all written in the atmosphere of controversy.[68] In spite of the fragmentary nature of the two treatises as they are left to us, it is clear that in both of these writings Pelagius is moved by anxiety lest he allow injustice to be attributed to God and lest he give way to a Manichaean doctrine of creation. These are fundamental worries which his proximity to Jerome have stirred in him, as was suggested above at the close of Chapter 2, and they inform such characteristic assertions as the following: if men "cannot" be without sin, then it is impossible to attach guilt to them;[69] an infant dying unbaptized is not condemned because sin is not contracted by birth;[70] sin is not a "substance" and therefore cannot cripple or transform human nature;[71] flesh and spirit are not contrary substances which, joined together by God, war against each other, nor does flesh impose upon man a natural necessity of sinning;[72] God is to be viewed on the model of a physician who comes to cure a wound after it has been inflicted, and we are not to think of him as creating man in such a way that there has to be a wound in order that there be health;[73] the idea of God's punishment for sin is absurd if that punishment turns out itself to be a weakening of the sinner with the express result that he commit more sins.[74]

In this series of assertions Pelagius seems implicitly to apply two corollaries to the governing ideas of God's justice and the goodness of creation: the notion of sin as a condition of birth must dissociate both guilt and moral responsibility from sin,[75] and there is no third alternative between sin as necessity imposed by the conditions of creation and sin as due exclusively to the activity of will. There is, to be sure, a certain kind of necessity imposed by habit, but this is a necessity which men have prepared for themselves. Pelagius' insistence that men can be without sin is an emphatic assertion of the doctrine of creation by a just God; it is nothing more, and it is nothing less.

Pelagius' famous distinction between *posse, velle,* and *esse,* the first of which is due to the gift of God and the latter two to human decision and action, is not to be understood as supplying an exhaustive vocabulary for the description of man's actual condition in the time of grace. The entire passage in which he formulates this distinction makes it clear that he is trying to do one thing: to defend his own doctrine of man's capacity for sinlessness against the charge that this capacity is one which men have apart from the grace of God.[76] I have tried to show that the doctrine in question concerns the fundamental nature of man as possessing a resource which at present is untapped. This doctrine in Pelagius' theological scheme does not immediately concern the redeeming work of Christ, does not concern the present necessity for the grace of the gospel. His opponents upon hearing the doctrine adopted one line of attack in assuming that it applied to this latter context and so raised the question of grace.[77] This in turn prompted Pelagius, who wished above all to be orthodox, to define as a gift of grace the capacity for sinlessness implanted in man by the Creator.

In like manner are we to understand what is perhaps Pelagius' most misleading statement: that men are able to fulfill the commandments of God *more easily* by grace.[78] It will not do to suppose that here in a defensive treatise from the year 416 he adopted a basically different position regarding the power of sinful habit from that which he had enunciated in his earlier years when faced with the task of Pauline exegesis. In the very work in which he makes the famous statement with its adverb *facilius* he also repeats at three different places the theme of the power of sinful habit, even designating that habit as holding a man by "a certain necessity." [79] The assertion in question is cast in its extreme form, I suggest, as a result of a problem of language in which Pelagius was fatefully caught. He had chosen to speak of the capacity for sinlessness by employing prominently the verb *posse* and the noun *possibilitas*.[80] These words had been useful to him in denoting a property of that enduring nature in which man is created; they were useful within the context of that problem in which Pelagius was chiefly interested through the course of the controversy. But they were much less useful when a question was asked which did not belong to that context, viz., "What is the relation of the grace of the gospel to man's enduring *posse?*" He could not, without completely reforming his language, say that it is grace which brings it about that man "is able" to be without sin. The latter is what he must be interpreted as meaning, apart from the requirements of his vocabulary concerning the nature of man. But he could not say it, and instead he said that men "are able more easily by grace" to obey the commandments of God. Pelagius was not a notably adroit theologian in the midst of controversy.

Christ as Redeemer, Revealer, and Example

The commentary on Paul reflects a number of traditional ways of speaking of the redeeming work of Christ. Christ is, for example, a pure sacrificial offering to the Father,[81] or he has manifested his eternal life in our flesh to the end that it might become immortal.[82] Pelagius' most characteristic and oft-repeated language specifies Christ as dying an undeserved death on behalf of men. The eternal Son, consubstantial with the Father, assumes human nature in both body and soul, and endures the condemnation of death that is due to men because of their sins. The death which he undergoes is not due to him both because as man he is without sin and because he is the Creator of the universe, hung upon the cross on behalf of his own creature. "Christ, then, for whom there was no judgment of death and no cause of enduring either the cross or curse, submitted to the curse for us, because we were all guilty of death; as standing under a curse we were deserving of the tree ourselves, in that we did not abide by all the things which were written in the law." [83] Thus are Christians preserved from the death that is due to them and to all men,[84] and thus is the Father's love made known.[85]

Christ is, second, the revealer. That which he reveals is the will and the promises of God for man; Pelagius can variously specify this aspect of the activity of Christ as "teaching," [86] the giving of commandments,[87] and the giving of "law." [88] It is of the greatest importance to be aware that in the mind of Pelagius there is no antithesis between the notions of gospel and law as such. Repeatedly he emphasizes that the term "law" applies to the new dispensation which Christ has brought. Grace is law,[89] the New Testament as a whole is law.[90] The Gospels are a *supplementum legis,* in which "examples and commandments for our living are most fully set down." [91] The difference between the law of Moses and the gospel is a difference between two laws. The nature of this difference is expressed in a number of ways. The law of Moses was written in hard stone, and the Jews had in their possession only tablets inscribed in their absence; in the gospel the Lord himself was present among men and gave them his law in their hearing; this law his hearers took into their hearts, and the Gospels were written down when the words of the Lord were still matter of living memory.[92] Or to speak in another way, Christ the physician has come in his own person, once man's disease had reached its most desperate moment, whereas before he had sent his medical students.[93] It is quite true, avers Pelagius, that the splendor of the law of Moses is emptied out into the splendor of the gospel, but this emptying out is to be understood as a progression: the child is "emptied out" into the man, and the seed into its fruit.[94]

And Christ is example. Pelagius understands this both in a general and in a specific sense. In a general sense it means that Christ offered to men the one paradigm case needed in the time of grace of a man who consistently put to death sinful desire and thus revealed to men that of which their nature is capable.[95] Specifically Christ serves as example for a number of concrete modes of behavior. By his taking upon himself the form of a servant and in remaining obedient unto death he teaches Christians the humility and obedience proper to themselves;[96] by his bearing of our infirmities we learn to bear with one another;[97] by his birth of a poor mother we learn to reject riches;[98] by his not "learning letters" he teaches us to reject worldly wisdom;[99] and so on.

Clarification is needed immediately of a confusion which might arise from the tripartite schematism by which the work of Christ has thus been described. Redeeming death, teaching, and example are *all* included under the single conception of the reconciliation which Christ has effected between God and man. Pelagius' words to this effect are regrettably of the briefest sort, but the fundamental assertion is clear. It is the death of Christ which allows the past sins of men no longer to bring upon them the condemnation of death, but it is the teaching and example of Christ which undo the effect of habit and open up to man the real possibility of a sinless life. Pelagius can write that God has reconciled us to himself "equally through the teaching and example of Christ." [100] *Doctrina* is the means by which peace is made between God and man.[101] It is by the example of Christ that Christians put to death the flesh.[102] There is at work here a conception which Pelagius never brings clearly to expression such that when the truth about human nature is clearly and finally presented to man in the teaching of Christ and in the example of his life, this truth has the power of penetrating through the layers of ignorance with which habit has overlaid human nature and of reviving that nature so that it may effectually assert itself. We shall return to this subject shortly. Here we may take note of Pelagius' comprehensive formula: Christ delivers us "by forgiving sins and by his teaching and by example." [103]

It will have been clear in all of the foregoing that there is a basic continuity both between creation and redemption and between the old and the new covenants. The continuity between creation and redemption Pelagius expresses in a way that is more easily conveyed in Latin than in English. By the sacrificial offering of his death Christ "repurchased" (*redemit*) us, he did not "purchase" (*emit*) us, since before his coming we were already his by reason of our nature, although alienated from him by our own sins.[104] We are reunited (*reconciliati*) to God, having already been united (*conciliati*) to him, again on the ground of our nature.[105] Having already been "generate" of him, we are now regenerate.[106] Such passages express the underlying continuity between creation and redemption, but they also point clearly to the contrast between "natural" and redeemed man *in the time of grace;* they speak eloquently of Pelagius' meaning when he employs the conception of human "nature": that with which all men are endowed by creation but which must be restored and re-established because of the effect of sins. Pelagius does not teach the doctrine that men by their own "unaided nature" may attain salvation; he teaches that men have the capacity to be without sin, which, as I have tried to show, is a different doctrine.

The continuity between the old and new dispensations of God, Pelagius emphasizes in a number of ways: in his continual polemic against Manichaeans and others who depreciate the Old Testament, in his use of the term "law," in his teaching that in the time of the law, the kingdom of heaven was open to those who obeyed the law of Moses, and in his frequent assumption that in acquiring knowledge of the will of God Christians should be acquainted with both the Old and the New Testaments.[107] Knowledge of the "law" in one sense is now just as incumbent upon Christians as, in a different sense, it was for the Jews before Christ.

The Grace of the Gospel

The threefold work of Christ in redemption, revelation, and example is grace as that work is received into the lives of Christians. The benefit of the redeeming death of Christ Christians receive as the forgiveness of sins in the sacrament of baptism. Grace in this sense justifies the ungodly and makes him to be "without sin." [108] Within this context of meaning justification is by faith alone;[109] in remitting our sins Christ makes us to be "righteous without our labor," makes us to be "acceptable and pleasing" (gratos) to himself.[110] Considered in relation to past sins, grace is the forgiving activity of God, whereby men are freed of guilt and pronounced wholly righteous.

But grace is also the help which comes of God through the teaching of Christ and his example.[111] Interpreters of Pelagius have sometimes been inclined to understand his doctrine of grace as "help" as if he really did have something like an incipiently Augustinian doctrine of grace.[112] Pelagius himself has perhaps given some encouragement to such interpretations by his willingness at the Synod of Diospolis to anathematize those who say "that God's grace and assistance is not given for single actions but consists in freedom of choice, or in law and teaching." [113] And in the work *On Free Choice* he can write that in addition to that freedom of choice implanted in us by the Creator, "we are fortified by his own daily help." [114] Whatever Pelagius may have intended at Diospolis,[115] it is possible to interpret both of these passages by what he explicitly says concerning the manner of the divine help. In this regard two fragments from his work *On Free Choice* are of decisive significance:

> We do not, as you think, confess the grace of God as consisting only in the law but also in the help of God. God helps us through his teaching and revelation, in that he opens the eyes of our hearts, in that he makes clear to us the things to come lest we be occupied in things of the present, in that he exposes the snares of the devil, in that he enlightens us with the manifold and unspeakable gift of heavenly grace.[116]

> And how will that saying of the Apostle stand secure, "It is God who is at work in you both to will and to bring to effect"? He works in us to will what is good and to will what is holy, in that he rouses us, by the greatness of the future glory and by the promise of rewards, from our devotion to earthly desires and from that love by which we delight only in the things of the present after the manner of dumb animals, in that by revealing wisdom he stirs our numbed will toward a longing for God, in that he persuades us toward everything which is good.[117]

Careful perusal of these fragments and comparison of them with others[118] leads to the conclusion that Pelagius conceives God's "help" to be essentially revelation by which man comes to know the things pertaining to his final salvation. Eminent among these things are the rewards and punishments which await men in the judgment. God "helps" by revealing in Scripture that "wisdom" which pertains to man's fundamental nature and to his obligation before God. By this revelation the mind is illumined and the will is stirred in such a way that the ignorance and paralysis brought on by prolonged habit are overcome and the will of God may again be obeyed. This liberating function of grace applies of course to Christ's entire work as revealer and example. Pelagius' teaching in this regard he sums up himself in a brief note on Rom. 6:14: "The grace by which we conquer has offered us teaching and example." [119]

We might capture Pelagius' whole teaching on the grace of Christ as "help" in a single formula: Christ by the example of his life, by his commandments, and by his teaching concerning man and God has brought the final revelation of that "way" [120] for man which leads to life and in doing so has brought "help" sufficient to overcome the power of sinful habit.

The doctrine of the work of the Spirit which Pelagius enunciates is quite fragmentary, but so far as it goes it parallels in a striking way his language about grace. The Spirit shows us the will of God and makes plain the future glory so that we may desire heavenly things and not earthly. The latter activity is characterized as "illumination" by which our weak *possibilitas* is aided.[121]

It is possible now to summarize the whole doctrine of grace. "Grace" means to Pelagius the following: (1) that original endowment with rational will by which men have the capacity to be without sin; (2) the law of Moses; (3) the forgiveness of sins in virtue of the redemptive death of Christ; (4) the example of Christ; (5) the teaching of Christ, conceived both as "law" and more generally as teaching concerning the things proper to man's nature and salvation.

Pelagius has no doctrine of grace other than this. It would be unfaithful to the man himself to attempt to save his "orthodoxy" by reading in some doctrine of infused grace which is not there. In an expository note which is distressingly brief but nonetheless clear in its implication, he lets it be known that it is precisely this doctrine of grace, as offering unambiguously clear knowledge of the will of God, which both affirms the divine "help" and preserves man's freedom of choice.[122] His fundamental conception of the nature of man and of man's ailment would not easily be synthesized with such a doctrine of grace as has characterized

Western Catholic theology. He conceives man's nature to possess a fundamental structure of rationality and attunement to the divine will which remains intact and unaltered by the effect of habitual sin. What man needs in order that he may effectively recover his own nature is, objectively, revelation; subjectively, knowledge—knowledge that is so authentic, clear, and compelling that the cloud of ignorance which presently hides his nature from himself will be done away. This knowledge is given to him in Scripture: in law, teaching, and example. Pelagius requires a doctrine of grace which will allow human nature, which has never been crippled or even weakened, to stand out clearly revealed; by thus emerging in its own clarity it will be able to resume its effective working.

Georges de Plinval has written of the "mysterious and saving intervention of grace . . . divine intervention alone," [123] which Pelagius' teaching seems to posit. The only thing that is perhaps mysterious is that Pelagius could have attributed such a crucial role to teaching and example and to that "knowledge" by which Christians become aware of the same. But such is the doctrine of Pelagius. This is made more evident by our noticing the continually repeated emphasis which he places upon the acquisition of knowledge of Scripture. At a number of places in the Pauline commentary he reveals his enduring preoccupation with the theme of *scientia,* whether it be that "natural knowledge" by which man as created was to know God, or whether it be that knowledge of the "law" by which man now may know the will of God.[124] It is "as knowledge increases" that our salvation is nearer than when we first believed.[125] Pelagius interprets Phil. 1:6 as meaning not that it is God who has "begun a good work" among the Philippians but the Apostle Paul, and the good work in question is said to be either that of teaching or of dispensing the "grace of knowledge." [126] In two of his letters of counsel Pelagius is at pains to make the point that knowledge of the will of God comes before the doing of that will; doing is indeed finally more important than knowing, but in point of time knowledge is prior.[127] It is the commandments of the law in both Old and New Testaments by which access to life is opened up to us.[128] "Difficult" is it that anyone should be saved without "knowledge of the divine law." [129] "The beginning of obedience is the will to know what is commanded." [130] The divine law is an immense field luxuriant with flowers by which the mind of the loving reader is nourished and revived; the greatest assistance toward a righteous life is to fill the mind with the divine sayings, to be continually exercised in meditation upon the sacred writings.[131] And finally we may recall that the very first item of teaching for which Pelagius was called to answer at the Synod of Diospolis was the sentence from his book of testimonies: "No man is able to be without sin unless he has acquired knowledge of the law." [132]

BAPTISM, JUSTIFICATION, AND THE CHRISTIAN LIFE

Pelagius' teaching concerning baptism may be summarized conveniently by saying that it is the sacrament of justification by faith alone.[133] Interesting it is that Pelagius can not infrequently supply the adjective *sola* to *fides* in this connection and thus go even beyond the Apostle in the terms by which he states the sufficiency of faith.[134] Faith he seems clearly to understand as not simply intellectual assent but "trust from the whole heart";[135] faith is also "faith in the promises of God." [136] In the act of baptism the believing man is absolved from his past sins without respect to merit, the forgiving grace of God making him to be in that moment "righteous." Righteousness in this context then means the condition of being without the guilt of past sins; the man who believes in Christ has the status of one who has fulfilled the whole of the law.[137]

In the teaching on baptism there reappears a crucial role assigned to *doctrina*. Commenting on Eph. 5:26 in the commentary, Pelagius writes as follows: "Water has washed the body, teaching [*doctrina*] has cleansed the soul, as he [Paul] says to the Hebrews: 'Having cleansed your hearts from an evil conscience, and washed your bodies with pure water'; in like manner you should also cleanse the bodies of your wives by continence and their souls with teachings." [138] These words point in two directions: toward Pelagius' basic understanding of the way in which God works his influence upon the rational creature, and toward the admonitions in letters of counsel that his correspondents be pure in both body and soul.[139]

Pelagius reveals the train of thought lying behind such a brief comment on baptism in his letter concerning knowledge of the divine law addressed to a young Roman nobleman. There his argument can be formulated in the following steps: in baptism sins are graciously forgiven, but this takes place only with the consent and will of the believer who signifies in the act of baptism his intention to obey the divine commandments; grace cannot be thought to impose itself and its effect upon man's will, otherwise the nature of will is violated; consent, will, and obedience are proper only to incorporeal soul; that which is incorporeal issues only from that which is incorporeal, just as the corporeal issues from the corporeal; the corporeal can be purged only by the corporeal, and the spiritual by the spiritual; "it is manifest that obedience comes from the moral intention of the soul, not from corporeal stuff";[140] the water of baptism, therefore, cleanses the body (presumably from the stain which it has contracted through involvement in sins) and it is the *word* (i.e., the "word of life," Eph. 5:26) which cleanses the soul.[141]

In this interesting way does Pelagius extend his basic conception of man into his thought concerning baptism. In his doctrine of creation, on the one hand, he sets off rational will against any "necessity" whether it be necessity imposed by the natural order or necessity to obey the will of God. Here, on the other hand, he sets will off against any improper understanding of grace such that will ceases to be

itself, and he circumscribes the rational and believing soul
as being inaccessible to the cleansing activity of water. This
dual achievement he accomplishes by the notion of "word,"
or of *doctrina*. " 'Word' is incorporeal"; it speaks, as it were,
to the soul; in accord with the will of the believer, it cleanses
the soul; in the word does the soul find its "glory." [142] Pelagius is saying that in the word or *doctrina* which accom-
panies baptism the soul is freed from the guilt of sins and
has restored to itself the effectual capacity of obedience to
the law of God. The only alternative which he considers to
this teaching is that which would suppose baptism to find its
whole significance in the washing with water, which would
mean that man "believes with his body." [143]

Not the least significant aspect of the argument here is
that it occurs within a context in which Pelagius has just
announced the theme of the Incarnation: the Lord who is
the Word of God has descended from the heavens and has
assumed human nature in order that mankind, lying fallen
in the following of Adam, might be raised up in Christ.[144]
It is, then, the very Word of God himself who cleanses the
soul at baptism and in whom the man of faith believes with
his whole heart. Pelagius' doctrine of man and man's will,
his doctrine of grace, and his doctrine of the person and
work of Christ may therefore be seen to converge. Christ is
the incarnate Word consubstantial with the Father. As Word
of God to man he speaks the *doctrina* which is the will of
God for man, is himself the exemplification of the divine
way for man, and suffers the death by which man's sins are
forgiven. Honoring the freedom of the rational will which
he has created, he delivers man from the ignorance in which
habitual sin has buried human nature and again places that
nature at man's effective disposal.

Related to the theology of baptism and conversion are
three problems which may be raised with a view to the consistency of Pelagius' total teaching. We shall consider them
in ascending order of seriousness. First, it is well known that
Pelagius associated predestination with foreknowledge. One

might at first sight understand Pelagius to mean the following: God foreknows the future faith of those who will believe and on this basis "calls" them or "separates" them from those who would not choose to believe. His occasional language would seem to give support to such an interpretation.[145] But if this means that God actively implants faith in those who he foreknows will respond positively to the gift of faith, then this is not the teaching of Pelagius. He has no doctrine of the divine implanting of faith; faith owes its origin to the activity of free choice, as we shall see below. But Pelagius' language in this respect is misleading for a second reason. As will be indicated below, he is not infrequently at pains to argue that faith is only the beginning and that justification in the fullest sense is not by faith alone but by faith followed by works of righteousness. Repeatedly he urges his correspondents so to act that they will merit the heavenly rewards, and he warns of the dire consequences of not doing so.[146] He obviously writes with the assumption that some, perhaps many, who have believed will not enter the kingdom of heaven. It would be quite trivial, on Pelagius' terms, to suppose that the divine initiative in choosing some and rejecting others should be based upon foreknowledge of their *faith*, rather than, say, their performance of works of righteousness.

To understand Pelagius properly, therefore, it is necessary to lay emphasis first upon his identification of predestination with foreknowledge: "to predestine is the same as to foreknow." [147] This particular formulation I take to mean that God's predestination is nothing but foreknowledge of those who will believe and who on the basis of their faith will be supplied with grace sufficient to do the divine will. By this identification therefore he removes any thought that God's choosing and calling take place in violation of the nature of freely chosen faith. But Pelagius himself can ignore the identification of the two terms and can speak of God as predestining in the sense of laying down an ordered structure of things: appropriate rewards follow upon their respective merits; empowering grace is given to the man of faith.[148] This entire theme is not a prominent one in the writings of Pelagius; he is to be seen as attempting to make intelligible within his own scheme the Pauline language of "predestination." His reading of Ambrosiaster provided him with the association of predestination with foreknowledge.[149] The most illuminating observation which he makes on the subject is his comment that the Apostle speaks of predestination in order to counter "the enemies of faith, lest they judge the grace of God to be fortuitous";[150] by grace as "fortuitous" Pelagius would mean, as we shall see, grace given to those not exhibiting the faith which may receive it. Although it is a delicate procedure to reduce his various comments to a single formula, God's foreknowing predestination in Pelagius appears to mean two things: (1) God's will to make his grace available to those who he knows will come to him in faith;[151] (2) God's will that future rewards be commensurate with moral achievement in this life.[152]

There is then the problem of the origin of faith and of the "merit" attaching to faith. Pelagius frequently gives expression to the idea that justification by faith alone takes place without respect to human merits, and can also speak of "deserving" the grace of God by the "merit" of faith.[153] Here is no real problem in respect of Pelagius' own consistency, although his language is perhaps misleading.[154] It must be remembered that he conceives the power of sin to be a power over what man concretely *does;* sin is particular act, and sins are particular acts of disobedience to the law of God. That man is justified freely apart from merit means that he is accounted guiltless before God even though his actions have brought guilt upon him. The power of sin over concrete actions is not a complete power over the inner motions of mind, soul, or will. The only analysis which Pelagius provides of this entire problem is one in which, commenting on the Apostle Paul, he sees the fundamental problem to man as being posed by the law of Moses. That law in the time of grace produces within man the paralyzing schism by which he recognizes sin to be sin and even wills to be without it but is unable to bring his will to effect. When the fullness of God's law breaks through to man in the person and teaching of Christ, the same rational will which even under the old law desired to be free of sin possesses now freedom sufficient to the positing of faith in Christ. Faith "merits" grace in the sense that it is the indispensable and freely chosen condition of the effectual working of grace. Faith is not "act" in the decisive sense in which act under the old law either brought guilt or established "merit." Nor does faith itself work the forgiveness of sins; it is God who graciously forgives sins when the believer comes to him in trust.[155] Whether this, within the context either of the fifth or of the twentieth century, is a theologically acceptable account of faith in its relation to grace, it is fortunately not our business here to say.

There is a final issue in relation to baptism on which Pelagius is in serious difficulty with himself. His reflection upon the sacrament of Christian initiation is built on the model of adult baptism and makes scarce sense if baptism is administered to infants. In baptism sins are forgiven, and this must take place "with the consent and will of the believer." [156] The activity of grace presumes the "merit" of faith, and faith itself presumes the activity of free choice. Now Pelagius in express words makes clear that infants "do not yet make use of the choice of rational will"; it is on this ground that he can abjure the opinion of Celestius that infants are in the same condition as Adam before the fall.[157] Yet baptism is to be administered to infants and with the same formula of words as in the case of adults,[158] which clearly implies that for infants, too, baptism is said to be *in remissionem peccatorum*.[159] "Who indeed," Pelagius writes, "is so impious as to forbid the common redemption of the human race to an infant of any age?" [160] Nowhere does Pelagius show that he was able to adjust or to refine his theological language in such a way as to offer an intelligible rationalization for speaking of redemption and the remission of sins as applied to infants. His entire anti-Manichaean theology, with its concentration upon the rational will as free over against any and every external necessity, comes to grief when confronted with the sacramental practice of the Christian Church, a practice which he wished to uphold.

We have seen that Pelagius teaches the justification of the sinner by faith alone in the act of baptism. He also teaches that men are justified by works. The key to understanding his language is to notice that the formula "faith alone" applies to the unique situation of the individual at his conversion and baptism.[161] "Righteousness" (*iustitia*) as a term applying to the Christian after baptism, and pre-eminently at the judgment, is unthinkable without the performance of "works of righteousness," i.e., without obedience to the moral precepts of Christ and of the Apostles. When the Apostle, referring to justification in this wider sense, writes that "man is justified by faith apart from works of the law" (Rom. 3:28), he means to say that man is justified apart from ceremonial works of the law such as circumcision and the observance of new moons and Sabbaths, not apart from works of righteousness.[162] The whole of the Christian life as it is stretched out between baptism and the judgment is one in which Christians avail themselves of the grace of teaching and example; always exercising that freedom of choice which has been made effectual by grace, they obey the precepts of the gospel and so merit the rewards of the final kingdom of heaven.[163] Pelagius sums up his whole teaching on faith in its relation to righteousness in the following words: "Faith in the first instance is reckoned as righteousness for this reason, that [a man] is absolved as to the past, justified as to the present, and prepared for the future works of faith." [164]

It remains to be repeated that the foregoing has been a specialized study in the teaching of Pelagius. While I hope I have not greatly distorted a line of thought which for Pelagius was clearly of fundamental importance, I have removed this line from a bundle which is more complex and inter-woven than the above would perhaps suggest. The line delineated does represent, I think, the integrating cord which binds all else together. But I have not given attention here to Pelagius' Trinitarian thought, to his Christological arguments, to his notion of the Church, to his moral and ascetic teaching, nor have I conveyed the urgency and dra-matic quality which attach to his words on the judgment and wrath of God.

A question raised at the beginning remains unanswered: Does Pelagius' teaching on freedom and grace have for his larger theological scheme a like importance to that which it had for the controversy surrounding his name? The answer must be indirect. The idea of freedom, as he understood it, is of fundamental importance to his total scheme. Grace is defined as *doctrina* and *exemplum* in such a way that that freedom of choice is not destroyed but is preserved and lifted up so that it may be itself. Which is to say that the doctrine of redemption is framed to fit the requirements of the doc-trine of creation. Here, undoubtedly, is Pelagius' own deep-est motive for his insistence upon the full deity of the Son. It is none but the Creator who has come to man in redemp-tion, the Father and Son share *una operatio*—he makes these points a number of times.[165] And for him this would mean that the Redeemer cannot conceivably violate the structure of that human nature which he has created. Here the Trini-tarian motif converges with the anti-Manichaean motif. Created human will is free from any necessity external to it-self. Such will is implanted in man at creation, goes under-ground but is not destroyed in the course of human history, and emerges again in its own effectual working through the restoring activity of Christ. We may say that what the con-troversy did was to move Pelagius to draw an even firmer line between creation and redemption by defining man's created freedom as itself a gift of grace. The grace of crea-tion, then, fixes man's rational will in such a way that it is free of natural necessity, whereas the grace of redemption frees that same will from the necessity that it has prepared for itself. And likewise both the grace of creation and the grace of redemption operate in such a way that human will is never moved irresistibly by any necessity emanating from the will of God, except the necessity that will be will and therefore free. Whether or not his opponents were aware of what he was doing, Pelagius with this final stroke extended and yet clarified the structure of his own theology.

Author's Notes

Author's Notes

Chapter 1: INTRODUCTION

1. James Sellers, *Theological Ethics* (New York and London, 1966), p. 130.

2. Erich Fromm, *Psychoanalysis and Religion* (New Haven, Conn., 1950), p. 49.

3. *Ibid.*, p. 35. Fromm does go on to specify that the correlate to obedience in authoritarian religion is a view of man "conceived as being powerless and insignificant." That Pelagius has no such view of man means equally that he cannot be cited as exemplifying Fromm's "authoritarian" religion. Fromm's two types simply do not fit the contrasting theologies of Augustine and Pelagius.

4. John Ferguson, *Pelagius: A Historical and Theological Study* (Cambridge, England, 1956); Gerald Bonner, *St. Augustine of Hippo* (London and Philadelphia, 1963), pp. 312–93; Georges de Plinval, *Pélage, ses écrits, sa vie, et sa réforme* (Lausanne, 1943).

5. Chapter 6, on the theology of Pelagius, was written before I saw H. H. Esser's article "Thesen und Anmerkungen zum exegetischen Paulusverständnis," *Studia Patristica* VII (*Texte und Untersuchungen* XCII, Berlin, 1966), pp. 443–61. If I had been aware of it at the time of writing, the chapter would not have been affected in any substantial degree. Esser is chiefly concerned with a comparison between the theology of Paul and that of Pelagius, which is not really my concern in that chapter. I have seen only advertisements of Gerald Bonner's article "How Pelagian was Pelagius? An examination of the contentions of Torgny Bohlin," *Studia Patristica* IX (*Texte und Untersuchungen* XCIV).

Chapter 2: PELAGIUS AND THE REVIVAL OF THE ORIGENIST CONTROVERSY

1. Jerome, *In Hieremiam* (CCL 74), prolog. 4: "stolidissimus et scottorum pultibus praegravatus"; *Dial. adv. Pel.* (PL 23) 3.16: "testitudineo incedens gradu."

2. See, for example, the treatment of John Ferguson, *Pelagius* (Cambridge, 1956), 77–81; the following is typical (p. 79): "Jerome . . . is for ever chasing the spectre of *apatheia*, and the ghosts of Origen and Jovinian mock him from the pages of Pelagius."

3. Henry Chadwick, *The Sentences of Sextus* (Cambridge, 1959), 121.

4. For the date, see Ferd. Cavallera, *Saint Jérome, sa vie et son oeuvre* (Louvain and Paris, 1922), II, 55.

5. See Jerome, *In Hiezechielem* (CCL 75), preface to Book 14.

6. Jerome, *Ep.* 133. See Cavallera II, 55.

7. *Dialogus adversus Pelagianos*, PL 23, 495–590.

8. Orosius, *Lib. apol.* 4: "beatus Hieronymus . . . in epistola sua, quam nuper ad Ctesiphontem edidit, condemnavit, similiter et in libro *quem nunc scribit*, collata in modum dialogi altercatione confutat." In chap. 7 of the same work Orosius states that the Jerusalem conference, at which he gave the testimony here quoted, had been held forty-seven days before the first day of the Feast of the Dedication in that year, i.e., on July 28. For the date of Jerome's *Dialogus*, cf. Cavallera, II, 55.

9. Jerome, *In Hier.* 1.17.3, 1.46.2, 1.56, 2.5.2, 2.51.2, 2.83.3, 2.96, 3.60.3, 3.70.4, 4.3.4, 4.41.4, 4.41.6, 4.48.4, 4.53.2, 4.60.3–6, 5.5.3, 5.37.2, 5.61.6, 5.66.12, 6.6.4, 6.29.11, 6.38.8.

10. *In Hier.* 3.1–3.

11. *In Hier.* 4.1.4: ". . . canes eos iuxta Isaiam esse mutos, qui latrare nesciant habentes quidem voluntatem et rabiem mentiendi, sed artem fingendi et latrandi non habentes." For Pelagius as dog see also *In Hier.* 3.1.3 and 4 and *Ep.* 50.1. For Pelagius as simply reproducing past calumnies see *In Hier.* 4.1.3: "Qui . . . veteres magistrorum suorum calumnias concinnantes in tantum elingues et miseri demonstrati sunt, ut ne maledicere quidem suis verbis potuerint"; also 5.61.6 and Prolog. 3–5.

12. *In Hier.* Prolog. 3: "Ut nuper indoctus calumniator erupit, qui commentarios meos in epistulam Pauli ad Ephesios reprehendendos putat . . ."; also 4.41.6.

13. *In Hier.* Prolog. 4, and 3.60.3.

14. Jer., *Comm. in Hier.* Prolog. 4: "Quae iste quasi sua profert, et alio iam calumniante purgata sunt."

15. Jer., *Ep.* 48.

16. *In Hier.* Prolog. 5.

17. *In Hier.* Prolog. 4, 4.1.2, 4.41.6–7, 5.61.6, 5.66.12. *Ep.* 133.3. *Dial. adv. Pel.* Prolog. 2, 1.19, 2.24. See also the repeated statements that the teaching of Pelagius represents a "nova ex veteri heresis": *In Hier.* 1.17.3, 1.46.2, 1.56, 5.5.3, 6.6.4.

18. Rufinus, *Apologia contra Hieronymum* (CCL 20), 1.23–44.

19. Jerome, *Ep.* 84.2.

20. See, e.g., Ruf., *Apol.* 1.22.

21. Ruf., *Apol.* 1.22: ". . . et quem in praefationibus tuis alterum post apostolos ecclesiarum magistrum dixisti, nunc haereticum dicas? Quis haereticus ecclesiarum magister aliquando dici potuit?" Cf. Jerome's preface to his translation of Origen's homilies on Ezekiel (GCS 8, 318): "ut Origenem faciam latinum et hominem iuxta Didymi videntis sententiam alterum post Apostolum (*apostolos* probably the correct reading) ecclesiarum magistrum etiam Romanis auribus donem." Thus what Jerome had written was not quite as emphatic as Rufinus would have it be; Jerome was passing on the opinion of his teacher Didymus, while showing no signs of disagreeing with it.

22. See Rufinus, *De adulteratione librorum Origenis* (CCL 20, 7–17).

23. *Apologia adversus libros Rufini* (PL 23, 397–492), 1.15–17 and 21–29, 3.11 and 13.

24. Jer., *Apol.* 1.16, 3.11.

25. Jer., *Apol.* 1.25: "Lege Graecos commentarios, et nisi ita repereris, crimen fatebor"; 1.27: "Nisi haec eadem in Graeco repereris, quidquid dictum est, meum putato."

26. Jer., *Apol.* 3.11: ". . . aperte confitentes quae sunt haeretica, quae catholica."

27. Jer., *Apol.* 1.25.

28. Jer., *Apol.* 1.21 and 25. Cf. *Comm. in Ephesios,* Prolog. (ad fin.) (PL 26, 412).

29. Jer., *Apol.* 1.1 and 3. Jean Steinmann, *Saint Jérome* (Paris, 1958), 290, confuses Rufinus' Apology against Jerome with his *Apologia ad Anastasium* and thus wrongly makes it appear that Jerome in the second book of his work is replying to Rufinus' *Apologia contra Hieronymum.* See Jerome, *Apol. adv. Ruf.* 2.1. Steinmann (pp. 289–93) adopts a far too indulgent attitude toward Jerome's Apology, although rightly bringing out the persistent insecurity which Jerome felt in the face of opposition in high places toward his translation of the Old Testament based on the Hebrew text.

30. Cf. Jer., *Apol.* 1.15–17 and 21–29 with 3.11 and 13.

31. Cf. e.g., the following passages: Jer., *Comm. in Eph.* 1.2.7; *Apol.* 1.24; and Ruf., *Apol.* 1.37. Jerome claims that in the commentary he was clearly offering three points of view—those of himself, Origen, and Apollinaris—and that the charge against him must be the trivial one that he has referred to Origen as *diligens lector.* Rufinus' point, on the other hand, has nothing to do with epithets applied to Origen but is, rather, that the reader naturally comes away from Jerome's remarks on Eph. 2:7 with the impression that Jerome is teaching the salvation of the devil and his angels.

32. Cf., e.g., the following: Jer., *Comm. in Eph.* 1.1.4; *Apol.* 1.22; Ruf., *Apol.* 1.26–28. Rufinus claims that Jerome's words, "Alius vero qui Deum iustum conatur ostendere," imply that God's justice has not been defended in the preceding comments and that Jerome is therefore putting forward, as Catholic defense of the divine justice, the teaching which follows on the premundane existence of souls. Rufinus further goes beyond the credible in suggesting that if Jerome now denies responsibility for this teaching, he is thus denying the justice of God. See also Ruf., *Apol.* 1.33–36 and cf. Jer., *Comm. in Eph.* 1.1.12.

33. Cf. the favorable judgment given on Rufinus by Cavallera (II, 97 ff.) in his Note, "L'Exactitude de Rufin." Whereas Cavallera is certainly correct in his general position in contrast to the modern revival of accusations against Rufinus by J. Brochet (*Saint Jérome et ses ennemis*, Paris, 1906) and George Grützmacher (*Hieronymus*, 3 vols., Berlin, 1901–8), he is, I think, not sufficiently critical of Rufinus. Cavallera's position is in general followed by F. X. Murphy, *Rufinus of Aquileia* (Washington, D.C., 1945), pp. 140 ff.

34. Jer., *Apol.* 1.16 and 3.11. Cf. *Ep.* 84.2.

35. *Ep.* 84.2.

36. *Commentarius in Ecclesiasten*, CCL 72, 249–361. For the date see M. Adriaen in his preface to this edition of the work, p. 248.

37. Jer., *Comm. in Eccl.* 1.9–10: "videtur mihi de his . . . nunc communiter loqui, quod nihil sit in natura rerum, quod non ante iam fuerit."

38. Jer., *Comm. in Eccl.* 1.9–10: ". . . fuit ergo homo, antequam sub sole fieret." Cf. Origen. *De princ.* 3.5.3.

39. Jerome's text at Eccles. 1:10: "Estne verbum—de quo dicatur, vide hoc novum est—iam fuit in saeculis, quae fuerunt ante nos." Jerome believes this text to have been made more intelligible by Symmachus as follows: "Putasne est—qui possit dicere: Vide hoc novum est, iam factum est in saeculo—quod fuit ante nos." See the whole passage on pp. 256–58, CCL 72.

40. Jer., *Comm. in Eccl.* 1.10: "Cum superioribus autem congruit

quod nihil novum in mundo fiat; nec sit aliquis, qui possit existere et dicere, ecce hoc novum est; siquidem omne quod se putaverit novum ostendere, iam in prioribus saeculis fuit."

41. Jer., *Comm. in Eccl.* 4.2–3: "Alii vero hunc locum ita intellegunt."

42. Jer., *Contra Ioannem Hierosolymitanum* (PL 23, 355–96), 7. Here the second proposition reads as follows: "Secundum, quod in hoc corpore quasi in carcere sint animae religatae; et antequam homo fieret in paradiso, inter rationales creaturas in coelestibus commoratae sunt."

43. E.g., *Comm. in Eccl.* 4.13–16 (Gregory Thaumaturgus and Apollinaris).

44. E.g., *Comm. in Eccl.* 4.2–3, 5.1–2, 12.5 (Apollinaris).

45. Cf. the much different impression of Jerome's use of Origen in the *Comm. in Eccl.* given by Steinmann, 181–85. In view of the evident quotations at 1.9–10 and 4.13–16 and the explicit naming of Gregory before the second of these, it is difficult to understand how Steinmann can write, concerning Jerome's use of other commentaries (p. 183): "Sans les citer, il parle de ceux d'Origène, de saint Grégoire le Thaumaturge, de Victorinus."

46. For the date, see Cavallera, I, 139 f. and II, 27. The commentary on Galatians intervened.

47. Jer., *Comm. in Eph.* 2, Praefat: "et interdum per singulos dies usque ad numerum mille versuum pervenire . . . ."

48. Jer., *Comm. in Eph.* Prol. (ad fin.): "Illud quoque in praefatione commoneo, ut sciatis Origenem tria volumina in hanc epistolam conscripsisse, quem et nos ex parte secuti sumus. Apollinarium etiam et Didymum quosdam commentariolos edidisse, e quibus licet pauca decerpsimus, et nonnulla, quae nobis videbantur, adiecimus sive subtraximus, ut studiosus statim in principio lector agnoscat, hoc opus, vel alienum esse, vel nostrum." Cf. *Comm. in Gal.*, Prolog: ". . . imbecillitatem virium mearum sentiens, Origenis commentarios sum secutus."

49. Jer., *Comm. in Eph.* 1.1.12. Jerome's text of the verse reads: "Ut simus in laudem gloriae eius, qui ante speravimus in Christo." Jerome writes that it would have been one thing if St. Paul had said only that we have hoped in Christ, but now "praepositionis adiectio ad illam nos intelligentiam trahit, de qua superius disputavimus." Cf. 1.1.4 and Rufinus' remarks, *Apol.* 1.31–32. Jerome chooses not to deal with this passage in his Apology.

50. Jer., *Comm. in Eph.* 1.2.15.

51. Jer., *Comm. in Eph.* 1.2.15: "hominem iuxta imaginem et similitudinem Dei factum, eandem post reconciliationem formam re-

cepturum, quam et nunc angeli habent, et ipse perdiderit." Cf. the eighth of the eight points as formulated in Jer., *Cont. Ioan. Hier.* 7: "Octavum, quod extremum obiicit, imaginem et similitudinem Dei, ad quam homo conditus fuerat, dicit ab eo perditam et in homine post paradisum non fuisse."

52. Ruf., *Apol.* 1.40–1. Cf. Jer., *Apol.* 1.23 and *Ep.* 124.4. It is true that Jerome in the same commentary, 2.4.16, speaks of the view that "omnes in angelos reformentur" as a "heresy." Here, however, that clause is carelessly posited as the equivalent of "omnes in una aetate sint positi," i.e., Jerome is combating the view that there will be in the world to come no hierarchical ordering of the rational creatures. Earlier in the same passage he says that all the rational creatures are to be understood under the image of one living rational being ("sub unius rationabilis animalis . . . exemplo") whose presently separated members will be marvelously joined together. Note also that at 2.4.16 Jerome seems clearly to speak of the restitution of the *angelus refuga*; cf. Jerome's reckless defense of this passage in *Apol.* 1.27, and Rufinus' remarks in his *Apol.* 1.44 f.

53. Note that in regard to the text at hand Jerome writes, *Comm. in Eph.* 1.2.15: "Et hanc totam intelligentiam ad angelos virtutesque coelestes et ad *animas* temperabit humanas." Cf. *Cont. Ioan. Hier.* 7: "Quintum, quod carnis resurrectionem membrorumque compagem . . . apertissime neget" See also Jer., *Ep.* 84.5 f.

54. Jer., *Comm. in Eph.* 1.2.7 (cf. Ruf. *Apol.* 1.37 and Jer., *Apol.* 1.24) and 2.4.16 (cf. Ruf., *Apol.* 1.44 f. and Jer., *Apol.* 1.26). This is the third item in the eight-point indictment—see Jer., *Cont. Ioan. Hier.* 7.

55. Cavallera, I, 138, n.2.

56. See, e.g., *Comm. in Gal.,* Prolog (PL 26, 308B).

57. On these points see Cavallera, I, 138–42, with notes and references there given. On Jerome's view of the obscurity of Ephesians, see the prologue to his *Commentary* (PL 26, 441A and 442A).

58. Steinmann, 190, accepts Jerome's defensive view in the *Apologia* of his attitude to Origen in the commentary on Ephesians, but without argument and without citation of passages.

59. Cavallera, II, 121–25. Jerome's *Ep.* 70, from the year 397, can both call Rufinus by the epithet *Calpurnius Lanarius* (c.6) and can say the following of Origen (c.4): "Christianorum et philosophorum inter se sententias comparans et omnia nostrae religionis dogmata de Platone et Aristotele, Numenio Cornutoque confirmans."

60. See the references to Origen in the writings of Jerome's last years collected by Cavallera, II, 125–27.

61. See chap. 4, below.

62. Jer., *Comm. in Hier.* 1.17.3, 1.46.2, 1.56, etc.

63. On Jerome's previous relations with Pelagius, see chap. 3, below.

64. Jer., *Comm. in Hier.* 3.1.2: "... id agit diebus et noctibus et aperte et per insidias veris falsa miscendo, immo universa mendacia subdolo melle circumlinens. ..."

65. On Pelagius' residence in Rome, see Georges de Plinval, *Pélage, ses écrits, sa vie, et sa réforme* (Lausanne, 1943), p. 64.

66. See F. X. Murphy, *Rufinus of Aquileia* (Washington, D.C., 1945), pp. 91 and 205.

67. CCL 20, 285 and Murphy, 213.

68. Palladius, *Historia Lausiaca* 118.

69. As one may gather from his *Epistola ad Demetriadem* (PL 30, 15–45) and his letter to a young and recently converted member of a senatorial family, *De divina lege* (PL 30, 105–16).

70. For Pelagius on the island of Sicily, see section I of my monograph *Four Letters of Pelagius* (New York, 1968). For Pelagius briefly in Africa, see Aug., *De gestis Pelagii* 46.

71. See Bohlin, pp. 83 ff.; cf. Souter 1, 183 ff.

72. See chap. 3, below.

73. "The Commentary of Pelagius on 'Romans' Compared with that of Origen-Rufinus," *J.T.S.* xx (1918), 127–77.

74. Torgny Bohlin, *Die Theologie des Pelagius und ihre Genesis* (Uppsala and Wiesbaden, 1957), 77–103.

75. Alexander Souter, ed., *Pelagius's Expositions of Thirteen Epistles of St. Paul*, Texts and Studies ix.2 (Cambridge, 1926).

76. Souter 1, 188.

77. See chap. 6 of this book.

78. See Murphy, 186; and Souter 1, 4 f.

79. Anastasius, *Ep. ad Simplicianum* (PL 22, 772–74) 3: "quaedam capitula blasphemiae ... quae nos non solum horruimus et iudicavimus, verum et si qua alia sunt ab Origene exposita, cum suo auctore pariter a nobis scias esse damnata"; *Ep. ad Venerium* (PL Suppl. 1, 791 f.): "... Origenes ... a nostris catholicis pectoribus habeatur alienus."

80. Anastasius, *Ep. ad Ioann. Hier.* (ACO 1.5, 3 f.): "... beatissimorum principum nostrorum manasse responsa, quibus unusquisque Deo serviens ab Origenis lectione revocetur; damnatumque sententia principum, quem lectio reum profana prodiderit."

81. Jer., *Ep.* 143. Aug., *Ep.* 202.

82. Aug., *De grat. Chr.* 2. It was in fact in response to the entreaties of the family of Pinianus that Pelagius made his most emphatic statement on grace as continuing, necessary help (*ibid.*): "Anathemo qui vel sentit vel dicit, gratiam Dei qua Christus venit in hunc mundum peccatores salvos facere, non solum per singulas horas, aut per

singula momenta, sed etiam per singulos actus nostros non esse necessariam; et qui hanc conantur auferre, poenas sortuantur aeternas."

83. Aug., *De gratia Christi et de peccato originali,* 1.1. For details and references on this family group see W. H. Fremantle in DCB iii, 888 f. and H. Leclerq in DACL xi.i, 209–30 (the latter to be used with caution).

84. See Jerome, *Ep.* 133.1, 3, 8, 10; *Dial. adv. Pel.* I.1, 2, 15, 16, etc.

85. See A. J. Smith's articles in *J.T.S.* xx (1918), 55–65; and xxxi (1930), 21–35; and Bohlin, 46–56.

86. See chap. 4, *ad fin.*

87. Bohlin sees this direction of Pelagius' thought clearly and was in fact the first to give prominent place to it in a theological analysis of Pelagius. But he goes too far in attempting to organize the whole of Pelagius' theology around an anti-Manichaean polemic. See, e.g., p. 16 in his book and cf. Plinval, *Pélage,* 217.

88. Cf. Bohlin, p. 56: "Bei Pelagius begegnete [Augustinus] der Fragestellung und den Begriffen seiner Jugend, dem, wovon er sich selbst in hartem Kampf losgerungen hatte, in stark ausgeprägter und verallgemeinerter Form." See below, chap. 5., *ad fin.*

89. Jer., *Ep.* 133.8, 10; *Dial. adv. Pel.* Prolog. 2; 1.15, 16, 19, 23.

90. *Dial. adv. Pel.* 1.18; 3.13.

91. *Ibid.,* 3.4; cf. 1.18 and 2.30.

92. *Ep.* 133.3; *Comm. in Ier.* 4.41.4 (CCL 74, p. 211). On the question of the identity of this Sextus, see chap. 4 of this book.

93. *Dial. adv. Pel.* 1.19.

94. *De lib. arb.* (frag. Souter 2, PL Sup. I, 1541 f.).

95. *Dem.* 27 (42B). Hereafter this letter will be cited as *Dem.*

96. *Dem.* 26; *Cel.* 56 (340 f.).

97. *Dem.* 27 (41C–D).

98. Jer., *Dial. adv. Pel.* 1.19. See *Virg.* 7 (233, 2) and *Exp.* 319, 17.

99. *Cel.* 6; *Lib. fid.* 6; cf. *Virg.* 7 (233).

100. Cf. Pel. in Aug., *De nat. grat.* 37, where he complains that certain people have accused him as follows: "comparari hominem deo si absque peccato esse asseratur."

101. *Dial. adv. Pel.* 1.16 and 21.

102. See Souter's fragments of *De libero arbitrio* in PL Sup. 1, 1539–43. For *De natura,* see Aug. *De nat. et grat.* 8: "ego dico posse esse hominem sine peccato. tu quid dicis?, etc."; *ibid.* 63. I am not claiming that Pelagius had read Jerome's dialogue (being written in the summer of 415) before writing *De natura* (to which Augustine responded some time in 415). Rather, it would seem to be the case that both Jerome's dialogue and Pelagius' *De natura* were parallel works which grew out of conversations between the two camps. Whether Pelagius

and Jerome confronted each other in Palestine is impossible to say. Jerome does show in his *Dialogue* (e.g., 1.10, 1.11, 1.12, 1.14) that he is able to produce authentically Pelagian arguments, whereas Pelagius clearly shows familiarity with arguments used by Jerome; see, e.g., *De Nat.* (Aug., *De nat. et grat.* 60) and *De lib. arb.* (frag. Souter 1, 1539) and cf. Jer., *Ep.* 133.9.

103. For reff. to Pelagius' two treatises, see chaps. 5 and 6.

Chapter 3: THE CRITIC OF JEROME'S TEACHING ON MARRIAGE

1. Jerome, *In Hier.* Prolog. 4: ". . . ut praeteream contra Iovinianum volumina, in quibus dolet virginitatem nuptiis et nuptias digamiae et digamiam polygamiae esse praelatam." *Ibid.*, 3.60.3: "Unde superflua novi heretici reprehensio, qua docuimus digamiam et trigamiam non ex lege descendere, sed ex indulgentia." S. Reiter, the editor of *In Hier.*, supposes Jerome to be referring to Jovinian by the words "novi heretici" (CCL 74, 154). It is much more likely that the reference is to Pelagius, because (1) this passage is clearly related to the above passage at Prolog. 4, (2) Pelagius at 5.5.3 is clearly referred to as "novus hereticus," and (3) Jerome several times in this commentary points to the teaching of Pelagius with the words "nova heresis": 1.17.3, 1.46.2, 1.56, 2.5.2, 6.6.4.

2. Jer., *In Hier.* Prolog. 4: ". . . dolet virginitatem nuptiis et nuptias digamiae et digamiam polygamiae esse praelatam."

3. Pel., *Epistola ad Demetriadem* (hereafter designated as *Dem.* and to be found in PL 30, 15–45), 9 (24)

4. Pel., *Exp.* 170, 15–171,2; 496, 1–11.

5. Pel., *Lib. fid.* 10 (1718): "Exsecramus etiam eorum blasphemiam . . . qui primas nuptias cum Manichaeo, vel secundas cum Cataphrygis damnant."

6. Jer., *In Hier.* 3.60.3. See note 1 above.

7. Jer., *Ep.* 133.4; *In Hier.* 3.60.3; *Dial. adv. Pel.* 1.25.

8. Jer., *Adv. Iov.* 1.14–15. Pel., *Exp.* 170, 15–171, 2; 496, 1–11.

9. Pel., *Exp.* 496, 1: ". . . necesse est ut quae tales sunt ante hoc faciant quam illut promittant, unde si transgressae fuerint, damnentur."

10. Cf. Jerome's comments, *In Hier.* 4.60.3: "Et quia solent semper heretici prospera polliceri et caelorum regna peccatoribus pandere . . . decipiuntque blanditiis miseros, et maxime mulierculas oneratas peccatis, quae circumferuntur omni vento doctrinae . . . ."

11. See Pel., *Exp.* 496, 6.

12. Jer., *In Hier.* 4.41.6; *Ep.* 133.3; *Dial. adv. Pel.* Prolog. 2, 2.24.

13. See Wilhelm Haller, *Iovinianus* (Texte und Untersuchungen N.F. ii, 2, Leipzig, 1897), 132–59.

14. Jer. *Ep.* 133.3; *Dial. adv. Pel.* 2.24.

15. Jer., *Adv. Iov.* 1.3: ". . . eos, qui plena fide in baptismate renati sunt, a diabolo non posse subverti."

16. See Haller, 132–42. Haller is no doubt right in interpreting as roughly equivalent for Jovinian the three formulae "a diabolo non posse subverti" (see Jer., *Adv. Iov.* 1.3), "a diabolo non posse tentari" (see *ibid.* 2.1), and "non posse peccare" (see *ibid.* 2.35). It seems clear that Jovinian supported his second proposition with texts on "not sinning" from 1 John, i.e., 3:9 f. and 5:18, the latter of which of course would give him scriptural ground for correlating "not sinning" with being invulnerable to "the evil one" (see Jer., *Adv. Iov.* 2.1).

17. See Julian in Aug., *Opus imperfectum contra Iulianum* 1.98.

18. See, for example, the following passages: Pel., *Exp.* 34, 9–22; 340, 11–341, 3; 400, 5–15; *De vita Christiana* (hereafter designated as *Vita* and to be found in PL 40, 1031–46) 10 and 13; *De virginitate* (hereafter designated *Virg.* and to be found in CSEL 1, 225–50) 6 (230–32); and the passages excerpted from *De natura* in Aug., *De natura et gratia*, 33–43.

19. Pel., *Libellus fidei* (PL 45, 1716–18) 13: "et tam illos errare qui cum Manichaeis dicunt hominem peccatum vitare non posse, quam illos qui cum Ioviniano asserunt hominem non posse peccare."

20. Jer., *Adv. Iov.* 1.3.

21. Jer., *Ep.* 48.1 and 49.2.

22. Jer., *Ep.* 50.3.

23. Jer., *Ep.* 49.13 (this letter is so numbered in the Hilberg edition, CSEL 54, but is numbered 48 in the Vallarsi edition, PL 22).

24. Jer., *Adv. Iov.* 1.7. That Jerome under pressure to explain himself, is not able to provide an entirely consistent interpretation of his words on this point is clear from a comparison of this passage with two others: *Ep.* 49.14 and 17.

25. Jer., *Adv. Iov.* 1.26.

26. Jer., *Adv. Iov.* 1.7, and cf. *Ep.* 49.15. See below, nn. 98 and 106 for evidence that Jerome takes some of his more extreme thought and language from Tertullian, *De Monogamia*. For a judicious appraisal of the *Adv. Iov.*, see Cavallera I, pp. 156–64, with notes.

27. Jer., *Ep.* 50 (CSEL 54, 388–95) 5: "Nunc libere et inpudenter iactat in vulgus et perstrepit: 'damnavit nuptias.' "

28. Georges de Plinval, *Pélage, ses écrits, sa vie, et sa réforme* (Lausanne, 1943), 53.

29. John Ferguson, *Pelagius* (Cambridge, 1956), 77 f. Ferguson (p. 77) and Plinval (p. 53, n. 2) both seem to think that this identification

was considered and rejected by D. Vallarsi, the eighteenth-century editor of Jerome. In the passages of Vallarsi's *Vita S. Hieronymi* to which they both refer, however (PL 22, 90), this precise point is not considered. The two questions which Vallarsi does entertain and which he answers in the negative are: (1) whether Pelagius was one of the persons whom Jerome had especially in mind when he wrote his letter to Pammachius (*Ep.* 48) defending *Adversus Iovinianum,* and (2) whether Pelagius is properly to be considered a *discipulus* of Jovinian. Ferguson makes a further mistake (p. 77) in asserting that W. Haller in his book on Jovinian "suspends judgment" on the identification of Pelagius with Jerome's unnamed monk. Haller makes no mention of this possibility; he considers, only to reject, the notion that the monk is to be identified with Rufinus of Aquileia (see Haller, *Iovinianum,* p. 53, n. 1 and p. 54, n. 1).

30. J. N. L. Myres, "Pelagius and the End of Roman Rule in Britain," *Journal of Roman Studies* 50 (1960), 21–36.

31. Jer., *Ep.* 50.2: "Liberatus est mundus de periculo et hereditariae vel centumvirales causae de barathro erutae, quod hic forum neglegens se ad ecclesiam transtulit."

32. For this date see Cavallera, II, 43.

33. Jer., *Ep.* 50.1: ". . . de trivio, de competis, de plateis circumforanum monachum rumigerulum, rabulam, vafrum tantum ad detrahendum, qui per trabem oculi sui festucam alterius nititur eruere. . . ." Cf. *ibid.* 5: "Non est grande, mi Domnion, garrire per angulos et medicorum tabernas ac de mundo ferre sententias . . . ."

34. Pel., *De divina lege* (hereafter to be cited as *De lege* and to be found in PL 30, 105–16) 9 (115 C–D).

35. Aug., *De gestis Pelagii* (CSEL 42) 36 and 44; *De haeresibus* (PL 42) 88; Mercator, *Commonitorium adversus haeresim Pelagii,* Prolog. (ACO 1.5, p. 5).

36. Jer., *Dial. adv. Pel.* 2.25: "Et tu in medio vulgi, unusque de populo mundum esse te credis?"

37. Jer., *Ep.* 50, 1 and 3. Cf. the following two passages: *Ep.* 50.3: "audio praeterea eum libenter virginum et vidvarum cellulas circumire et adducto supercilio de sacris inter eas litteris philosophari"; and *Ep.* 53.7: "alii adducto supercilio grandia verba trutinantes inter mulierculas de sacris litteris philosophantur." The latter letter, to Paulinus of Nola on the study of Scripture, comes from about the same time as *Ep.* 50 and reflects Jerome's continuing worry.

38. The word used in *Ep.* 50 and in *Ep.* 133.4 is "mulierculae," which in the latter case forms part of a quotation from 2 Tim. 3:6.

39. Jer., *Ep.* 133.4.

40. Jer., *Dial. adv. Pel.* 2.24: "Ego etiam si mulierum vallor agminibus, nullam habeo concupiscentiam."

41. Jer., *Dial. adv. Pel.* 1.25: "Verum tu tantae es liberalitatis, ut favorem tibi apud amazonas tuas concilies . . ."; *In Hier.* 3.60.3: "nisi forte tribuit indulgentiam amazonibus suis, ut usque ad decrepitam senectutem bella libidinum experiantur."

42. *Ad Demetriadem* (PL 30, 15–45), *De vita Christiana* (PL 40, 1031–46), *De virginitate* (CSEL 1, 224–50), and *Ad Celantiam* (CSEL 56, 329–56).

43. Jer., *Dial. adv. Pel.* 1.25: "Scientiam legis etiam feminas habere debere"; *ibid:* "Quod et feminae Deo psallere debeant."

44. Jer., *Ep.* 50.2: "Inventus est homo absque praeceptore perfectus, πνευματοφόροϛ και θεοδίδακτοϛ."

45. Jer., *Dial. adv. Pel.* 1.29: ". . . restat ut non recte facias, qui indoctus usurpas scientiam scripturarum, et magister prius quam discipulus esse coepisti." Cf. Plinval, *Pélage,* 51, n. 4.

46. Jer., *Ep.* 50.2: ". . . cum praesentem Iovinianum . . . eloquentiae suae mole oppresserit."

47. Jer., *Ep.* 50.4: ". . . Iovinianum solus intellegit est quippe proverbium balbum melius balbi verba cognoscere."

48. Pel., *Exp.* 142, 11 f.; 409, 10–12; 421, 4. A fourth possible instance, at 281, 12, does not belong to the authentic text of Pelagius.

49. Jer., *Ep.* 50, the first part of §3 and especially the sentence "fateatur ergo publice quod domi loquitur."

50. Jer., *Ep.* 133.11: "Sola haec heresis est, quae publice erubescit loqui quod secreto docere non metuit"; *ibid.* (somewhat previously): "loquere quod credis; publice praedica quod secreto discipulis loqueris." See also *In Hier.* 4.1.5, and cf. Plinval, *Pélage,* p. 53, n. 3.

51. Jer., *Ep.* 50.3: ". . . lustrare nobilium domos, haerere salutationibus matronarum. . . ."

52. Pel., *De lege* 6.

53. Pel., *Dem.* 1. For details concerning the Anici family see Jerome, *Ep.* 130.

54. *Virg.* 14, 244; 16, 246; *Cel.* 21, 347.

55. Jer., *Dial. adv. Pel.* 1.29: "Nisi forte humilitate solita, magistrum tuum iactitas dominum, qui docet omnem scientiam, et cum Moyse in nube et caligine facie ad faciem audio verba Dei, et inde nobis cornuta fronte procedis."

56. I am indebted to Professor John T. Townsend of the Philadelphia Divinity School, for his help in unraveling this bit of Jerome's sarcasm.

57. Orosius, *Liber apologeticus* (CSEL 5, 603–63) 31: ". . . praeferens etiam in fronte pinguedinem . . . ."

58. Jer., *Ep.* 50.4: "habet latera et athletarum robur et belle corpulentus est."

59. Jer., *Dial. adv. Pel.* 1.28: "et Milonis humeris intumescis."

60. Jer., *Dial. adv. Pel.* 3.16: "testitudineo incedens gradu."

61. Jer., *In Hier.* Prolog.: ". . . stolidissimus et Scottorum pultibus praegravatus . . . ."

62. Jer., *In Hier.* 3.1: ". . . latrat [i.e., diabolus] per Alpinum canem, grandem et corpulentum . . . ."

63. Orosius, *Lib. apol.* 31: ". . . latos humeros gestas robustamque cervicem . . . ." Cf. Plinval, *Pélage,* p. 53, and Ferguson, pp. 77 f.

64. Jer., *Ep.* 50.4: "Quotiens me iste in circulis stomachari fecit et adduxit ad coleram, quotiens conspuit et consputus abscessit."

65. Jer., *In Hier.* 4.1.6: "Quodsi cavendum nobis est, me veterem laedere videamur necessitudinem, si superbissimam heresin spiritali mucrone truncemus, ergo sustinendae nobis erunt cruces proditae fidei . . . ."

66. Jer. *Ep.* 50.5: "Non aeque inter fusa et calathos puellarum et inter eruditos viros de divinae legis dogmatibus disputari."

67. See, e.g., *Exp.* 35, 14–17; 60, 20; 179, 2; 244, 16–245, 9. *De lege* 3 (107–8).

68. Jer., *Ep.* 50.5, especially the clauses "Moveat manum, figat stilum, commoveat se et, quidquid potest, scriptis ostendat," and "cum autem ad libros venerit."

69. See above, chap. 2, n. 76.

70. Aug., *Contra Iulianum* 2.36: "De illo quidem sancto presbytero [i.e., Hieronymo] . . . non solet Pelagius iactitare, nisi quod ei tamquam aemulo inviderit."

71. Jer., *Ep.* 50.5: "Inter mulierculas sciolus sibi et eloquens videbatur; postquam Romam mea opuscula pervenerunt, quasi aemulum exhorruit et de me quoque captavit gloriam."

72. See Cavallera, I, 84–91, with references there given.

73. Jer., *Ep.* 152 (CSEL 56, 364 f.). The letter is to be dated in 418, the year before Jerome's death; see Cavallera, I, 333 f. and II, 57 f. The adjective in the form "Pelagianae hereseos" occurs in *Ep.* 154.3 (CSEL 56, 368).

74. See chap. 4, below, for Pelagius' personal reputation. Jerome himself calls attention to his habit of not naming the authors of Pelagian teaching, "malens eos corrigi quam infamari." *In Hier.* 4.1.3.

75. Georges de Plinval, "Recherches sur l'oeuvre littéraire de Pélage," *Revue de Philologie* 40 (1934), 9–42; see also, by the same author, *Pélage, ses écrits, sa vie, et sa réforme* (Lausanne, 1943), and *Essai sur le style et la langue de Pélage* (Fribourg en Suisse, 1947).

76. C. P. Caspari, *Briefe, Abhandlungen und Predigten* (Christiania, 1890), pp. 3–167.

77. John Ferguson, *Pelagius* (Cambridge, 1956), pp. 186 f. and chap. 9.

78. P. L. Sup. 1, 1104 and 1375–1504.

79. John Morris, "Pelagian Literature," *J.T.S.* n.s. 16 (1965), pp. 26–60; see pp. 31 f. and 37–40 and cf. Plinval, "Recherches," p. 37.

80. See my monograph *Four Letters of Pelagius* (New York, 1968).

81. Morris, p. 40.

82. Caspari, pp. 122–67 = P.L. Sup. 1464–1505. Caspari's pagination, which will be used in the following reff., is reproduced in the Migne edition.

83. Serafino Prete, "Lo scritto pelagiano *'De castitate'* è di Pelagio?" *Aevum* 35 (1961), pp. 315–22.

84. *De cast.* 2, p. 123.

85. Prete, it must be admitted, overstates the contrast between the two authors. On this precise point Pelagius was able to write, *Exp.* 166, 22: "nuptiae enim peccatum non sunt, sed per sollicitudinem mundi qui nubunt legem servare vix possunt." The author of the *De castitate* was well acquainted with Pelagius' commentary on Paul (see my *Four Letters of Pelagius* [New York, 1968]), and intensified to an extreme degree rigorist lines of thought which are doubtless there in undeveloped form, while ignoring the more temperate tendencies. But whereas the unnamed author developed Pelagius' thought in an extreme, ascetic direction, Pelagius' own line of development was in the direction of the tempered position of the letter to Demetrias, upon which Prete chiefly builds his case (the commentary comes from the years immediately prior to 410, and the letter from the year 414). In this sense Prete's case is substantially correct.

86. See Prete, pp. 316–18, with references there given.

87. See Caspari, the whole of p. 142 and especially the following, where in commenting upon 1 Cor. 7:8 f. the author writes (p. 142): "Non dixit [i.e., Paulus]: ei deus illis hoc non donaverit nubant; quod eum dixisse convenerat, si hoc non spontaneae voluntatis sciebat esse, sed doni." For Pelagius on incontinence see *Exp.* 159, 9–11; 161, 3–7; 162, 21 f.; 489, 14–17; 496, 1–7 (note that the text of 496, 1 f. is as given above, n. 9). Here again, however, Pelagius in the commentary is not quite consistent, as can be seen by comparing the tendency of the passages just cited with *Exp.* 166, 21 f.

88. See my monograph *Four Letters of Pelagius* (New York, 1968).

89. Pel., *Exp.* 162, 17.

90. See especially *Exp.* 159, 7–11; 162, 21 f.; 166, 21 ff.

91. Caspari, p. 142. The scriptural text quoted is Sir. 15:18.

92. Prete, pp. 320–22, seems not to be aware of the Sicilian Briton's use of Pelagius' commentary

93. Celestin Charlier, "Cassiodore, Pélage et les origines de la vulgate paulinienne," *Studiorum Paolinorum Congressus Internationalis Catholicus,* 1961 (Rome, 1963), pp. 1–10; cf. Souter 1, pp. 245–64.

94. This MS is styled "V" in Souter's apparatus.

95. Pel., *Exp.* 159, 17 (incontinentiae re vera . . .)—160, 20 (. . . usus) and 160, 22 (corpus dicitur . . .)—161, 18 (. . . aliter).

96. Pelagius did not look with favor upon unilateral renunciation of sexual relations and expressed his disapproval explicitly in *Ad Celantiam* 28, 351 f.

97. Caspari, p. 142.

98. Caspari, p. 138; the Sicilian Briton was certainly familiar with Jerome's *Adversus Iovinianum;* the latter's sentence at 1.7 in comment on 1 Cor. 7:1, "Nihil enim bono contrarium est, nisi malum," is found exactly reproduced in *De cast.* 10.2, p. 138; also the sentence (*De cast.* 10.6, p. 142), "Suspiciosum bonum est, quod gravi poena melius aestimatur," undoubtedly reflects *Adv. Iov.* 1.9: "Suspecta est mihi bonitas eius rei, quam magnitudo alterius mali, malum esse cogit inferius." Jerome, in turn, throughout this section of *Adv. Iov.* is drawing upon Tertullian, *De monogamia* 3.

99. Pel., *Exp.* 489, 5–17, on 1 Tim. 4:2. *De cast.* (16, p. 159) also contains a paragraph citing the same passage from 1 Tim. in which they receive unfavorable mention, "qui ut malum nuptiae damnat," but this fact only serves to point up the tension between the author's loyalty to the language of Pelagius and the direction of his own thought. And it is to be noted, moreover, that the objects of his polemic are here identified specifically as Manichaeans and Marcionites who teach that there is one God of marriage and another of virginity. Cf. this paragraph with 10.7, p. 142, where it is said to be *illicitum* not to follow the apostolic counsel favoring virginity.

100. Jerome, *Adv. Iov.* 1.8 is willing to call marriage a "Dei donum," a view which the Sicilian Briton, familiar with Jerome's work (see above, n. 98), expressly rejects (*De cast.* 10.5, p. 142). Cf. also their contrasting remarks on the important Pauline verses, 1 Cor. 7:3–5; *Adv. Iov.* 1.7 and *De cast.* 10.4 (pp. 139 f.). Prete is not quite careful enough (pp. 319 ff.) in describing the views of the two authors on 1 Cor. 7 as "substantially identical." It is difficult to understand how Ferguson (p. 147), who believes Pelagius to be the author of the *De castitate,* can with equanimity write of "the moderate asceticism which he preached." Significant of something is the fact that Ferguson offers an appreciative interpretation of the work *De divitiis* (another of the tracts in the Caspari corpus and attributed to Pelagius by Ferguson following Plinval) but does not discuss the teaching on mar-

riage of the *De castitate* (see Ferguson, chap. 9 and especially pp. 147–53).

101. See Jer., *Adv. Iov.* 2.18–37.

102. See Jer., *Adv. Iov.* 2.4 f.

103. See Jer., *Adv. Iov.* 2.30 f.

104. Pel., *Lib. fid.* 6 and 12 (PL 45, 1717 f.). These remarks oppose Jovinian's first and fourth theses; see Jer., *Adv. Iov.* 1.3.

105. Pel., *Lib. fid.* 15 (1718); cf. Jovinian's second thesis (Jer., *Adv. Iov.* 1.3) and Jerome's discussion, 2.1–4.

106. Cf. Jer., *Adv. Iov.* 1.43, with Tert., *De monog.* 17; also cf. Jer., *Adv. Iov.* 1.15 with Tert. *De monog.* 5 (on the first and second Adams); cf. *Adv. Iov.* 15 ("exhibeant tertium Adam digamum") with *De monog.* 17 ("exhibe tertium Adam et hunc digamum"); cf. *Adv. Iov.* 1.15 with *De monog.* 11 (on remarriage as permissible only if one becomes a Christian as a widow); cf. *Adv. Iov.* 1.19 with *De monog.* 5 (on the example of Abraham); cf. *Adv. Iov.* 1.43 with *De monog.* 17 (on Lucretia, blotting out the stain of her rape by her own death). For Jerome's relation elsewhere in the *Adv. Iov.* to Tertullian's work, see above, n. 98.

Chapter 4: PELAGIUS AND THE SENTENCES OF SEXTUS

1. Aug., *De pecc. mer.* 3.6 and 14; *De gest. Pel.* 61; *De nupt. et conc.* 2.25 (referring to Julian of Eclanum but equally well applying to Pelagius); *Retract.* 1.8.3 and 1.8.4.

2. See Torgny Bohlin, *Die Theologie des Pelagius und ihre Genesis* (Uppsala and Wiesbaden, 1957), pp. 46–103.

3. Augustine, *De natura et gratia* 77.

4. Henry Chadwick, *The Sentences of Sextus*, Texts and Studies, New Series, V (Cambridge, 1959). For a number of corrections to the text of a collection of Pythagorean sentences also published in the same volume, see by the same author "The Sentences of Sextus and of the Pythagoreans," *J.T.S.*, n.s. 11 (1960), p. 349. See also G. Delling, "Zur Hellenisierung des Christentums in den 'Sprüchen des Sextus,'" *Studien zum Neuen Testament und zur Patristik*, Texte und Untersuchungen 77 (Berlin, 1961), pp. 208–41.

5. See below, pp. 46 f.

6. In the above paragraph I have drawn upon Chadwick, pp. 138–62.

7. Origen, *Contra Celsum* 8.30 and *Comm. in Matt.* 15.3.

8. Chadwick, pp. 112–16, is certainly right in this contention as

over against the view of Gildemeister, Preuschen, and Harnack that Origen considered the author to have been a pagan (see references in Chadwick, *loc. cit.*).

9. Origen, *Hom. in Ezech.* 1.11. The maxim in question is no. 352: "It is dangerous to speak even the truth about God." Chadwick has discovered two other extant passages from Origen in which the same maxim is quoted: the preface to the *Commentary on the First Psalm* (Epiphanius, *Panarion* 64.7.3), and the preface to the fifth volume of the *Commentary on St. John* (*Philocalia* 5.1, ed. Robinson, p. 42, 11.27 ff.); see Chadwick, *Sentences*, p. 115 and *J.T.S.*, n.s. 11 (1960), p. 349.

10. Origen, *Comm. in Matt.* 15.3. The two maxims from Sextus are nos. 13 and 273. For a full discussion of Origen and the Sentences, see Chadwick, pp. 107–16.

11. For discussion and references see Chadwick, pp. 131–33.

12. Chadwick, p. 9: "Sextus in Latinum verti, quem Sextum ipsum esse tradunt qui apud vos id est in urbe Roma Xystus vocatur, episcopi et martyris gloria decoratus."

13. So Chadwick, p. 130.

14. Aug., *De nat. et grat.* 77: "Quis item Christianus ignorat, quod beatissimum Xystum Romanae Ecclesiae episcopum et Domini martyrem dixisse commemorat . . ."; *Retractationes* 2.68 (42): "in quo verba quaedam, quae velut Xysti Romani episcopi et martyris Pelagius posuit, ita defendi, tamquam re vera euisdem Xysti essent; id enim putaveram. sed postea legi Sexti philosophi esse, non Xysti Christiani."

15. I am assuming that the unnamed monk of Jerome's *Ep.* 50 is Pelagius; see chap. 3. In any case Jerome (*Comm. in Ier.* 4.1.6) in 414 speaks of his "veterem necessitudinem" with Pelagius, which most probably means that he had known Pelagius in Rome, where he had not been since 385. Augustine (*Ep.* 177, 2) speaks of Pelagius as having lived in Rome for a long time.

16. See, e.g., the list for the Pauline commentary given by Souter, p. 553.

17. *Exp.* 133, 13–134, 3; 137, 22–138, 2; 139, 15 ff.

18. The traditional attribution to Xystus is confirmed also by Greek citations from the maxims and by the Syriac translations, both of which of course are independent of Rufinus' Latin translation. See Chadwick, p. 130.

19. Aug., *Retractationes* 2.68 (42); full quotation above, n. 14.

20. Jerome, *Comm. in Ezech.* 6 (CCL 75, p. 236); *Ep.* 133, 3; *Comm. in Ier.* 4.41.4 (CCL 74, pp. 210 f.).

21. See Chadwick's whole discussion, pp. 117–37.

22. Chadwick has made such a comparison relatively easy by his publication in the same volume of a collection of Pythagorean max-

ims (pp. 84–94) and of the collection of Clitarchus (pp. 76–83), as well as by many references to the letter of Porphyry to Marcella. See pp. 138–62 and the notes on pp. 163–81.

23. See Chadwick's notes, pp. 163–81 and G. Delling, *op. cit.* (n. 4 above).

24. Jerome, *Ep.* 133.3.

25. In modern times Pelagius has been said to be essentially a Stoic (see, e.g., Ferd. Cavallera, *Saint Jérome, sa vie et son oeuvre* [Louvain and Paris, 1922], I, p. 323), and to have derived his thought from Druidic religion (see, e.g., J. W. Willis Bund, *The Celtic Church of Wales* [London, 1897], p. 108).

26. See Chadwick, pp. 122–25, for the fortunes of Sextus in the Western Church after the fifth century.

27. Jer., *Comm. in Ier.* 4.41.4 (CCL 74, p. 211): "per multas provincias legitur."

28. Jer., *Comm. in Ier.* 4.41.4 (CCL 74, p. 211): "maxime ab his qui ἀπάθειαν et impeccantiam praedicant."

29. Jer., *Ep.* 133, 3: "unde et vos plurima contra ecclesiam usurpatis testimonia."

30. See Cavallera, II, p. 55.

31. It is to be emphasized that this chapter is concerned only with the modest task of a comparison between Pelagius and the Latin Sextus. Background questions about the sources contributing to the thought and language of Sextus, as well as questions concerning other theological, philosophical and cultural influences upon Pelagius have here been suppressed.

32. S 1–5 and 8: "Fidelis homo electus homo est; electus homo homo dei est; homo dei est qui deo dignus est; deo dignus est qui nihil indignum deo agit; studens fidelis esse nihil quod deo indignum est agas. vere fidelis est qui non peccat." The English translation will of course have only the Latin text in view, to be found in Chadwick, pp. 13–63. Attention will not be directed to all instances in which Rufinus has either failed to understand the Greek or intentionally changed its sense.

33. *Exp.* 34, 9–19; *Vita* 13; *Cel.* 2 (331, 10).

34. See chap. 6 of this book and cf. *Exp.* 35, 21; 319, 21 f.; and *De lege* 2 (107B).

35. *Vita* 13: ". . . ut fidem quam habere se simulant, sine iustitiae operibus apud Deum sibi censeant profuturam." *Exp.* 348, 19: ". . . fidem operibus comprobare."

36. See, e.g., S 330, 378, 379, 382, 408.

37. *Virg.* 6 (230, 24 ff.): "Iustitia ergo non aluid est quam non peccare, non peccare autem est legis praecepta servare. praeceptorum

autem observatio duplici genera custoditur, ut nihil eorum quae pro-
hibentur facias, et cuncta quae iubentur implere contendas." See also
De lege 4 (109B) and *Dem.* 9 (24B).

38. Jerome, *Dialogus adversus Pelagianos* 1.25: "sine peccato esse
non posse, nisi qui scientiam legis habuerit"; 1.29: "sapientiam et in-
tellectum scripturarum, nisi qui didicerit, scire non posse"; *ibid.:*
"scientiam legis non usurpare debere indoctum."

39. Augustine, *De gestis Pelagii* 2.

40. *Dem.* 9 (24A–B). Note the verbs *disco* and *facere* and cf. the
text of S 290.

41. *De lege* 3 (107D) and 4 (108D). See also *De natura* (in Aug., *De
nat. et grat.* 19).

42. S 290: "ea quae oportet discere et ita facere, ne coneris facere
antequam discas."

43. S 123: "ratio quae in te est, vitae tuae ipsa sit lex."

44. *De libero arbitrio* (in Aug., *De peccato originali* 30): "Tunc
enim duce ratione cognoscebatur creator, et quemadmodum esset viven-
dum, scriptum gerebatur in cordibus, non lege litterae, sed naturae."

45. *Dem.* 8 (23B).

46. *Exp.* 32, 8; 57, 2 f.

47. *Exp.* 59, 17–20: "Interior homo est rationabilis et intellegibilis
anima, quae consentit legi dei; lex enim eius est rationabiliter vivere
et non duci inrationabilium animalium passionibus."

48. S 205: "omnis passio animi rationi eius inimica est." Cf. S 204,
206, 207.

49. S 35: "habes in te aliquid simile dei et ideo utere te ipso velut
templo dei propter illud quod in te simile dei"; S 398: "si scis a quo
factus est, et temetipsum agnoscis." Cf. S 442.

50. Pel., *De natura* (in Aug., *De nat. et grat.* 53): "Nam cum dicitur,
ipsum posse arbitri humani omnino non esse, sed auctoris naturae,
Dei scilicet; ecqui fieri potest ut obsque Dei gratia intelligatur, quod
ad Deum proprie pertinere censetur."

51. Pel., *De lib. arb.* (in Aug., *De grat. Chr.* 5): "Posse ad Deum
proprie pertinet qui illud creaturae suae contulit."

52. Bohlin, pp. 17 and 89 f.

53. Aug., *De nat. et grat.* 77.

54. S 27, 28, 351, 361, 362. Cf. S 25, 26, 30, which do offer some minimal affirmations about God.

55. S 44, 148, 354, 356, 358, 360.

56. Pel., *Exp.* 133, 13–134, 2; 134, 5 f.; 134, 17 f.; 137, 9–12; 137, 22–
138, 2; 139, 15 ff.; 346, 15 f.

57. Pel., *Exp.* 16, 20 ff.; 30, 5–9; 133, 20–134, 2; 346, 15 f.; 349, 6–17;
365, 9 ff. *De lege* 4 (109A–B). Cf. *Exp.* 13, 16–14, 11.

58. Pel., *Dem.* 20 (34C).

59. S 44 and 148.

60. S 381, cf. 45 and 48.

61. S 210a.

62. S 50, cf. 115.

63. S 204–7.

64. See, e.g., *Exp.* 64, 17 f.; 236, 16 f.; 268, 7 f.; 263, 14 f.; 423, 11.

65. S 49: "deus quidem nullius eget, fidelis autem dei solius."

66. S 114: "mali nullius auctor est deus."

67. For explicit reff. in *Exp.*, see Souter, p. 553. For the latest writings, see *De lib. arb.* (fragmenta Souter, PL Sup. I, 1539–43) and *Lib. fid.* 10 and 13 (PL 45, 1718).

68. See fragmenta Souter (PL Sup. I, 1539–43) and Aug., *De pecc. orig.* 14.

69. See *Dem.* 3 and *De lib. arb.* passim.

70. S 36: "libertatem arbitrii sui permisit hominibus deus sine dubio ut pure et sine peccato viventes similes fiant deo." Cf. S 82a and 255.

71. *De nat.* (in Aug., *De nat. et grat.* 8), *De lib. arb.* (in Aug., *De grat. Chr.* 5), *Dem.* 3.

72. *Dem.* 3 (18A).

73. *De lib. arb.* (in Aug., *De grat. Chr.* 5): ". . . cum dicimus hominem posse esse sine peccato, et confessione possibilitatis acceptae laudamus deum, qui nobis hoc posse largitus est. . . ."

74. S 58–60, 221, 222, 225, cf. 228.

75. S 225: "nefas est deum patrem invocare et inhonestum aliquid agere."

76. S 60: "vir castus et sine peccato potestatem accipit a deo esse filius dei." See Aug., *De nat. et grat.* 77.

77. *Exp.* 64, 17 f.; 268, 7 f.

78. *Exp.* 400, 17–401, 1: "sicut vos deus fecit, considerate enim cuius filii sitis . . . ;" cf. S 221: "cum filium te dei quis dicit, memento cuius te filium dicat."

79. *Virg.* 14 (244, 6 ff.): "ergo si dei filia es, vide ne quid eorum facias, quae deo patri incongrua sunt, sed *age omnia quasi filia dei.*" S 58: "dignus esto . . . eo qui dignatus est te filium dicere, et *age omnia quasi filius dei.*"

80. *Dem.* 17 (31B): "Quis enim non erubescat et metuat tanto patre agere aliquid indignum . . . ?" Cf. S 58 (quoted in n. 79). Cf. also *Dem.* 19 (33B–C); *Vita* 2 (1034) and 14 (1045).

81. Aug., *De nat. et grat.* 77.

82. Jer., *Dial. adv. Pel.* 3.14.

83. Aug., *De gest. Pel.* 16.

84. In my article "Pelagius' Veracity at the Synod of Diospolis,"

Studies in Medieval Culture, ed. John R. Sommerfeldt (Kalamazoo, 1964), pp. 21–30, I have argued that Pelagius' testimony in general at Diospolis is not such as would give surprise if Pelagius did in fact refuse to acknowledge his own words. For internal evidence on the *De vita Christiana,* see my monograph *Four Letters of Pelagius* (New York, 1968). For external evidence see my "Pelagius, Fastidius and the Pseudo-Augustinian *De vita Christiana,*" JTS, n.s. 13 (1962), pp. 72–98.

85. *Vita* 11 (1042): "Ille autem ad deum merito extollit manus, ille preces bona conscientia fundit, qui potest dicere, Tu nosti, domine, quam sanctae, quam innocentes, quam purae sint ab omni fraude et iniuria et rapina, quas ad te expando, manus; quam iusta, quam immaculata labia et ab omni mendacio libera, quibus tibi, ut mihi miserearis, preces fundo."

86. *De lege* 4 (109B).

87. Here is a partial list of the occurrences of the word in Pelagius: *Exp.* 195, 10; *Virg.* 12 (242, 7); *Dem.* 1 (16A–B), 2 (16C), 10 (26B and C), 13 (27D), 13 (28A), 17 (31A and D), 22 (36C), 23 (37D), 24 (38B); *Cel.* 21 (347, 6); *De lib. arb.* (in Aug., *De pecc. orig.* 30). Whereas *mores* tends to be the word for positive moral character formed by habit, *consuetudo* tends to appear when the negative effects of the "habit of sinning" are under discussion; see *Exp.* 59, 6; 59, 12; 90, 21; 164, 2; 319, 4; 336, 3; *Dem.* 8 (23C); *De lib. arb.* (in Aug., *De grat. Chr.* 43), *bis; De lib. arb.* (fragmentum Souter 1, P.L. Sup. I, 1540). For exceptions to this pattern see *Dem.* 13.

88. *Dem.* 17 (31D): "nunc ergo ad omnem morum perfectionem mentis aciem intende, et ad coeleste praemium coelestem vitam para."

89. *Dem.* 13 (28A–B).

90. S 54, 57, 66, 94, 181, 233.

91. *Exp.* 362, 10; 484, 6; 492, 5; 493, 8; 530, 18; cf. 1 Cor. 7:34 and *Virg.* 9.

92. *Dem.* 26 (41A).

93. Jer., *Ep.* 133, 3.

94. Jerome's *Ep.* 133 and Pelagius' *Ep. ad Demetriadem* both come from the year 414.

95. *Dem.* 27 (41C–D).

96. S 204.

97. S 388 and 389a: "quod fieri necesse est voluntarie facito; quod non oportet fieri nullo modo facias." Chadwick (p. 103) *may* be right in translating the Greek original of this maxim so as to give it a Stoic sense: "What you are compelled to do, do of your own free choice" (cf. the Greek, ὃ δεῖ ποιεῖν, ἑκὼν ποίει). Such a thought would have seemed puzzling and possibly repugnant to Pelagius as smacking

of that kind of "necessity" which he was keen to deny, but he would not have found it difficult to apply his own sense to the maxim. It is not clear to me, moreover, that the maxim in its original form must carry the Stoic meaning, particularly since ὁ μὴ δεῖ ποιεῖν in the maxim immediately following (389a) clearly bears a moral sense: ὁ μὴ δεῖ ποιεῖν, μηδενὶ τρόπω ποιει. Many of the maxims, of course, are grouped according to subject matter. This argument can cut both ways, however. It is not unnatural to give 388 a Stoic sense if it is taken together with 387: τύραννοϛ εὐδαιμονίαν οὐκ 'αφαιρεῖται.

98. *Dem.* 9 (24B–C), 15 (29C–D); *Vita* 10 (1039–40); *Virg.* 6 (230, 24–231, 1); *Cel.* 5 (333, 11–24); *De lege* 4 (109A). Pelagius understands the dominical command at Matt. 7:12 to be a brief but most adequate summary of *iustitia*. Cf. S 89.

99. See the following passages: *Dem.* 15 (30A), 16 (30A–C); *Virg.* 7 (232, 21–234, 7); *Cel.* 5 (333, 24–334, 2), 6 (334); *De lege* 5 (110A–D); *De nat.* (in Aug., *De nat. et grat.* 13). See chap. 5 for a discussion of Pelagius' reaction to Jerome's charge that he was teaching the Stoic doctrine of the equality of all sins.

100. S 9, 10, 11, 297.

101. S 359, 383, 408, cf. all the maxims 352–62 on speaking about God.

102. *Exp.* 447, 8 and 532, 19.

103. S 230–39.

104. *Exp.* 159, 7–17.

105. *Dem.* 9 (24D–25A); *Virg.* 1–2.

106. See *Exp.* 167, 17 ff.; 376, 18–377, 4; 378, 12 f.; 429, 14 f.

107. Omitting *Exp.* 159, 17–160, 20 and 160, 22–161, 18. See chap. 3.

108. *Cel.* 28–30.

109. S 230b and 232; *Exp.* 159, 7–17.

110. S 13 and 273. Cf. the suggestion of G. Delling (*op. cit.* above, n. 4), that Sextus was engaged in modifying a maxim such as that appearing in Porphyry (*Ad Marcell.* 34), which encourages the taking of one's own life for the purpose of saving the soul; Delling's suggestion is that Sextus wished to modify the extremism of such a maxim by giving it the meaning which he understood to be possessed by Matt. 5:29 f. and 18:8.

111. Pelagius understood Matt. 19:12 as simply referring to those who undertake the life of virginity; see *Exp.* 166, 7 f. and *Dem.* 9 (25A).

112. S 230a. The ambiguity of the crucial clause in both its Latin and Greek forms ("coniugium tibi refutare concessum est,"—"γάμον γὰρ διδωσίν σοι παραιτεῖσθαι") makes its precise meaning unclear, and I have given what appears to me its most probable interpretation. Chad-

wick (p. 99) appears to interpret it as meaning that married partners may mutually renounce their marriage.

113. *Cel.* 28–30.

114. S 240 and 428. Other maxims on food and drink: 109, 111, 265, 268–69.

115. *Dem.* 18 (32A).

116. Jer., *Dial. adv. Pel.* 1.29: "Christianum illius debere esse patientiae, ut si quis sua auferre voluerit, gratanter amittat."

117. S 15: "quicquid saeculi habes, etiam auferat tibi quis, non indigneris." Cf. S 17.

118. S 128, 404, 92, 118; cf. 127, 130, 272.

119. *Exp.* 42, 3–43, 2; 500, 12 ff.; 504, 9–12; *Dem.* 10 (26C), 29 (43B–D); *De lege* 8 (114A–C) and 9 (115B–C).

120. *Exp.* 42, 9–11.

121. *De lege* 8 (114A–B).

122. S 19, 115, 140. *Exp.* 134, 2; 258, 3; 370, 15 f.

123. S 82b and c, 266, 267, 330, 377–79, 382.

124. *Exp.* 203, 3–21.

125. *Exp.* 505, 4: "quod perfectionis est fundamentum." See also *Vita* 14 (1044) and *Virg.* 6 (231, 7 ff.).

126. S 228, cf. 226.

127. *Exp.* 197, 19 f., text acc. to MS V and modified (*impii* for *iniqui*) in light of Cassidorus (who knew the text represented by V) and the text of Sextus. For V representing the original text of Pelagius, see Celestin Charlier, "Cassidore, Pélage et les origines de la vulgate paulinienne," *Studiorum Paolinorum Congressus Internationalis Catholicus*, 1961 (Rome, 1962), pp. 1–10. An early redactor of Pelagius' commentary struck out the original quotation and substituted Mal. 2:10, probably under the influence of Jerome's polemic against the Sextine collection.

128. Marius Mercator, *Commonit. super nom. Caelestii* (ACO 1.5, p. 67).

129. S 182–84.

130. *Vita* 3 (1035). Cf. *Exp.* 19, 15 ff., and 154, 5 f.

131. *Dem.* 20 (34C–35B); *Cel.* 20 (346 f.); S 64.

132. *Dem.* 19 (33D–34A); *Virg.* 8 (234, 20 f.) and 17 (247 f.); *Cel.* 16 (342 f.); S 278, 279. Note the nouns *obtrectatio* and *obtrectator*.

133. *Dem.* 21 (35B–D); *Cel.* 11 (338, 7) and 17 (344); S 149.

134. *Dem.* 19 (33D–34A); *Virg.* 8 (234, 20 f.), 10 (238, 22–239, 6), 17 (248, 3–8); *Cel.* 11 (338, 7) and 16 (343 f.); S 409.

135. *Exp.* 121, 2; 388, 13; 413, 2; 436, 14; 447, 9 f.; 537, 1 f.; *Vita* 6 (1038); S 372, 374.

136. S 14, cf. 39.

137. *Exp.* 42, 13 f.; 202, 18 ff.; 212, 10 ff.; 257, 5 ff.; 319, 14 ff.; 340, 11 ff.; 368, 5 ff.; 373, 19–374, 3; 400, 10 ff.; etc. *Dem.* 30; *Vita* 10 and 13; *Virg.* 7; *Cel.* 9 (336, 18 ff.) and 31; *De lege* 7–9; *Ep. ad Innoc.* (in Aug., *De grat. Chr.* 34); *Lib. fid.* 6.

138. See the following maxims: 33, 34, 82 bc, 129, 176, 190, 194, 218, 219, 226, 244, 246, 292, 306, 309, 310, 311, 319, 402, 421, 423, 450.

139. S 35.

140. S 429.

141. S 7a, 82d, 376a, cf. 376b.

142. See Chadwick, p. 191, for references (σοφόϛ and σοφία).

143. Scc, c.g., *Vita.* Praef. and 1; *Virg.* 3 (227, 17), 4 (229, 7), 13 (244, 1).

144. *Exp.* 349, 5.

145. *De lege* 3 (108A–C) and 4 (108D).

146. S 271: "ex carne nil oritur bonum."

147. *De lib. arb.* (fragmentum Souter 1, p. 437; PL Sup. I, 1539 f.).

148. S 36: ἐξουσίαν πιστῷ ὁ θεὸϛ δίδωσι τὴν |κατὰ θεόν·καθαρὰν οὖν δίδωσι καὶ ἀναμάρτητον. "libertatem arbitrii sui permisit hominibus deus sine dubio ut pure et sine peccato viventes similes fiant deo."

149. Origen, *In Evang. Ioannis* 2.10 (Lomatsch, p. 122): Ἔστι τινὰ δόγματα παρ' Ἕλλησι καλούμενα παράδοξα, τῷ κατ' αὐτουϛ σοφῷ πλεῖστα ὅσα προσάπτοντα μετά τινοϛ ἀποδείξεωϛ ἢ φαινομένηϛ ἀποδείξεωϛ. καθ' ἃ φασι μόνον καὶ πάντα τὸν σοφὸν εἶναι ἱερέα, τῷ μόνον καὶ πάντα τὸν σοφὸν ἐπιστήμην ἔχειν τῆϛ τοῦ θεοῦ θεραπείαϛ, καὶ μόνον καὶ πάντα τὸν σοφὸν εἶναι ἐλεύθερον, ἐξουσίαν αὐτοπραγίαϛ ἀπὸ τοῦ θείου νόμου εἰληφότα·καὶ τὴν ἐξουσίαν δὲ ὁρίζονται νομίμην ἐπιτροπήν.

150. Diog. Laert. 7.121: μόνον τε ἐλεύθερον (scil. εἶναι τὸν σοφόν), τοὺϛ δὲ φαύλουϛ δούλουϛ. εἶναι γὰρ τὴν ἐλευθερίαν ἐξουσίαν αὐτοπραγίαϛ, τὴν δὲ δουλείαν στέρησιν αὐτοπραγίαϛ· εἶναι δὲ καὶ ἄλλην δουλείαν τὴν ἐν ὑποτάξει, καὶ τρίτην τὴν ἐν κτήσει τε καὶ ὑποτάξει, ᾗ ἀντιτίθεται ἡ δεσποτεία, φαύλη οὖσα καὶ αὐτή. I owe the discovery of this passage, and the one immediately above from Origen, to Rev. Dr. Richard A. Norris, of Philadelphia Divinity School.

151. Porphyry, *Ad. Marc.* 11: ἀνθρώπῳ δε σοφῷ θεὸϛ θεοῦ δίδωσιν ἐξουσίαν.

152. See Chadwick, pp. 143 ff. and 165.

Chapter 5: ON AUGUSTINE AND PELAGIUS

1. Aug., *De nat. et grat.* 21; *Ep.* 190.6.22; *De gest. Pel.* 61. All references here to the anti-Pelagian treatises and letters of Augustine are cited according to the text in CSEL, treatises in vv. 42 and 60, letters in vv. 34, 44, and 57.

2. Jer., *Ep.* 133.3; *Dial. adv. Pel.* 1.1.

3. Jer., *Ep.* 133.10; *Dial. adv. Pel.* 1.1; 1.2; 1.19, etc.

4. *De nat. et grat.* 37.

5. Karl Barth, *Kirchliche Dogmatik* I.1² (Munich, 1935), p. 208; II.1² (Zürich, 1946), p. 633.

6. Franz Diekamp, *Katholische Dogmatik*, ed. Klaudius Jüssen, 10th ed. (Münster, 1952), II, p. 127.

7. *De nat. et grat.* 62.

8. Michael Schmaus, *Katholische Dogmatik* III.2⁵ (Munich, 1956), p. 273.

9. Reff. given by Jean Rivière, "Hétérodoxie des Pélagiens en fait de rédemption," RHE 41 (1946), p. 7 n. 3.

10. Adolf von Harnack, *Lehrbuch der Dogmengeschichte* III⁴ (Tübingen, 1910), p. 166.

11. *Ibid.*, pp. 167 f.

12. *Ibid.*, pp. 188, n. 2; 195.

13. *Ibid.*, pp. 199 f.

14. *Ibid.*, p. 201.

15. *Ibid.*, p. 192.

16. Jean Rivière, "Hétérodoxie des Pélagiens en fait de rédemption?" RHE 41 (1946), pp. 5–43.

17. A. Souter, *Pelagius's Expositions of Thirteen Epistles of St. Paul*, 3 vols., Texts and Studies IX (Cambridge, 1922–31). Celestin Charlier, "Cassidore, Pélage et les origines de la vulgate paulinienne," *Studiorum Paolinorum Congressus Internationalis Catholicus*, 1961 (Rome, 1963), pp. 1–10.

18. Reff. given in my monograph *Four Letters of Pelagius* (New York, 1968).

19. Torgny Bohlin, *Die Theologie des Pelagius und ihre Genesis* (Uppsala, 1957).

20. ACO I.1.3, p. 9.

21. Cf. H. Chadwick, "Eucharist and Christology in the Nestorian Controversy," *J.T.S.* n.s. 2 (1951), p. 149.

22. See Aug., *Epp.* 175–77; *Contr. duas Ep. Pel.* 2.5. It is of course true that Celestius had been brought before the Carthaginian synod in 411 and that Augustine had not participated in that affair. Our contention here is not the absurd one that the Pelagians would have found no opponents in the Latin world had it not been for Augustine but, rather, that Augustine played the leading theological role in the final Western judgment upon Pelagius.

23. I am deliberately leaving out of account the question of Celestius, which would entail a separate investigation.

24. Fr. Loofs, "Pelagius und der pelagianische Streit," PRE 15, pp. 747–74; see pp. 761–63 for the above point. Cf. the supplement to the original article, PRE 24, pp. 310–12.

25. The enduring usefulness of Loofs' essay is all the more remarkable for the fact that he was able to use only the highly defective text of Pelagius' *Expositions* in *P.L.* 30.

26. Aug., *De dono persev.* 53; cf. *Confessions* 10.40.

27. See Bohlin, pp. 46–56.

28. Aug., *De nat. et grat.* 80.

29. *Retract.* 2.58: "Venit etiam necessitas, quae me cogeret adversus Pelagianam heresem."

30. Celestius is Pelagius' *discipulus;* see, e.g., *De gest. Pel.* 23.

31. Aug., *De pecc. mer.* 1.1; *De gest. Pel.* 25: "... multorum fratrum perturbatur infirmitas."

32. The theses at issue at the synod were as follows (v. Marius Mercator in ACO 1.5, p. 66; cf. *ibid.,* p. 6): (1) "Adam mortalem factum, qui sive peccaret sive non peccaret, moriturus fuisset"; (2) "quoniam peccatum Adae ipsum solum laesit et non genus humanum"; (3) "quoniam parvuli qui nascuntur, in eo statu sunt, in quo Adam fuit ante praevaricationem"; (4) "quoniam neque per mortem vel praevaricationem Adae omne genus hominum moriatur neque per resurrectionem Christi omne genus hominum resurgat"; (5) "quoniam lex sic mittit ad regnum caelorum quomodo et evangelium"; (6) "quoniam et ante adventum domini fuerunt homines inpeccabiles, id est sine peccato." With (1) cf. *De pecc. mer.* 1.2; with (2) cf. *ibid.,* 1.9; with (3) cf. *ibid,* 1.20 and 23; with (4) cf. *ibid.,* 2.49; with (6) cf. *ibid.,* 2.1 and 12.

33. Aug., *De gest. Pel.* 46.

34. Pel., *De nat.* (in Aug., *De nat. et grat.* 42–5); *Exp.* 45, 16–20.

35. E.g., *De nat.* (in Aug. *De nat. et grat.* 33 f.).

36. *Ibid.,* 10.

37. *Exp.* 45, 14–20; *Virg.* 7 (233, 3 f.). At the Synod of Diospolis Pelagius anathematized all who had ever held to the first five of the theses which had been in question at Carthage (see n. 32 above). I have argued elsewhere that Pelagius' testimony at Diospolis is to be treated with caution; see "Pelagius' Veracity at the Synod of Diospolis," in *Studies in Medieval Culture,* ed. John R. Sommerfeldt (Kalamazoo, 1964), pp. 21–30.

38. In Souter's text of the *Expositiones* these arguments are found in the comments on Rom. 5:15, pp. 46 f.

39. *De pecc. mer.* 3.2 and 5. The arguments, according to the original text are as follows (*Exp.* 46, 25–47, 13): 'Hi autem qui contra traducem peccati sunt, ita illam impugnare nituntur: "si Adae," inquiunt, "peccatum etiam non peccantibus nocuit, ergo et Christi iustitia etiam non credentibus prodest; quia similiter, immo et magis dicit per unum salvari quam per unum ante perierant." deinde aiunt: "si baptismum mundat antiquum illut delictum, qui de duobus baptizatis nati fuerint debent hoc carere peccato; non enim potuerunt ad filios transmittere quod ipsi minime habuerunt. illut quoque accidit quia, si anima non est ex traduce, sed sola caro, ipsa tantum habet traducem peccati et ipsa sola poenam meretur," iniustum esse dicentes ut hodie

nata anima, non ex massa Adae, tam antiqua peccata portet aliena. asserunt etiam nulla ratione concedi ut deus, qui propria peccata dimittit, imputet aliena.'

40. *De pecc. mer.* 3.2 and Pel., *Exp.* 46, 25: "Hi autem qui contra traducem peccati sunt."

41. *De pecc. mer.* 3.6: ". . . sciens hanc nescio quam esse novitatem, quae contra antiquam et ecclesiae insitam opinionem sonare nunc coeperit . . . ."

42. *De pecc. mer.* 3.1: ". . . sancti viri, ut audio, et non parvo provectu Christiani . . . ."

43. *De pecc. mer.* 3.6: "Haec ergo et alia, quae hunc sequuntur errorem, nimium perversa et christianae repugnantia veritati credo quod vir ille tam egregie christianus omnino non sentiat."

44. *De spir. et lit.*, 1.1; cf. *De pecc. mer.* 2.7, 8, 21.

45. *De spir. et lit.* 3.

46. *De spir. et lit.* 4.

47. *De pecc. mer.* 3.1.

48. *Exp.* 24, 15–17; 35, 14–17 (continuity of new law with old); 58, 4 f.; 60, 20; 196, 9–15; 226, 5 f.; 244, 16–245, 9; 339, 5; 326, 4 f.; 389, 2; 408, 10–15; 453, 3 f.; etc.

49. *Exp.* 15, 16; 88, 19 f.; 128, 3–5; 215, 7; 453, 4; 480, 6 f.; etc.

50. *De spir. et lit.* 4.

51. *De spir. et lit.* 23–25; cf. Pel., *Exp.* 32, 4–6; 34, 17–19; 315, 15–18. Cf. Ambrosiaster (PL 17, 79A and 80D) and Jerome, *Comm. in Gal.* 1.3.2 (PL 26, 348).

52. The text of the entire letter (Aug., *Ep.* 146) is as follows: "DOMINO DILECTISSIMO ET DESIDERANTISSIMO FRATRI PELAGIO AUGUSTINUS IN DOMINO SALUTEM. Gratias ago plurimum, quod me litteris tuis exhilarare dignatus es et certum facere de salute vestra. retribuat tibi dominus bona, quibus semper sis bonus, et cum illo aeterno vivas in aeternum, domine dilectissime et desiderantissime frater. ego autem etsi in me non agnosco praeconia de me tua, quae tuae benignitatis epistula continet, benivolo tamen animo erga exiguitatem meam ingratus esse non possum simul admonens, ut potius ores pro me, quo talis a domino fiam, qualem me iam esse arbitraris."

53. Cf. Wilfrid Parsons, trans., *Saint Augustine, Letters*, III, "Fathers of the Church," vol. 20 (New York, 1953), p. ix.

54. Aug., *Ep.* 140.28–37. For further allusions to matters related to the Pelagian controversy in Augustine's letters of the years 412–415, see the following: *Ep.* 145.3 and 8; 149.21; 155.12.

55. The points are stated in concise form in Hilarius' letter, Aug., *Ep.* 156.

56. The first is given by Jerome as one of the headings in Pelagius'

Liber eclogarum (*Liber testimoniorum*), *Dial. adv. Pel.* 1.32; after the Synod of Diospolis, Pelagius claimed that this precise thesis had been approved by that synod, a claim that is less than accurate; see Aug., *De gest. Pel.* 54 and cf. *ibid.*, 16; see my comments in "The Veracity of Pelagius at the Synod of Diospolis," *Studies in Medieval Culture*, ed. John R. Sommerfeldt (Kalamazoo, 1964), pp. 28 f. The fourth of the above theses appears in Pelagius' letters, e.g., *Virg.* 7 (233, 13).

57. *Exp.* 128, 12; 484, 3; 515, 12. At Diospolis he was faced with this point and replied that by it he means two things: (1) that the laver of baptism washes away every spot and wrinkle; (2) that the Lord wishes the Church to remain in this condition (see Aug., *De gest. Pel.* 28).

58. Aug., *Ep.* 157.40.

59. See Pel., *De nat.* (in Aug., *De nat. et grat.* 10).

60. He goes so far as to say (*Exp.* 505, 2 ff.) that obedience to the dominical summons at Matt. 19:21 is the *fundamentum perfectionis.*

61. The extant writings of this figure are to be found in C. P. Caspari, *Briefe, Abhandlungen und Predigten* (Christiania, 1890), pp. 3–167. See the following: John Morris, "Pelagian Literature," *JTS*, n.s. 16 (1965), pp. 31 f. and 37–51; my monograph *Four Letters of Pelagius* (New York, 1968), and above, chap. 3.

62. Orosius took a copy of Augustine's letter to Hilarius with him to Palestine and read it out to the synod at Jerusalem in the summer of 415; Pelagius was then asked to say whether he taught the doctrines against which Augustine had written (Orosius, *Lib. apol.* 3 f.). It is unlikely that Orosius, sent to the Holy Land by Augustine, would either have had the letter with him or would have read it to the synod if the Bishop of Hippo had not been curious as to whether Pelagius really taught the theses in question. This, however, is matter of *inquiry*, not of accusation, as is made clear by even Orosius' biased account.

63. Aug., *Ep.* 157.6.

64. See n. 62 above.

65. Aug., *Serm.* 293.10–11.

66. Aug., *Serm.* 294.19: "Parum est enim quia isti disserunt, et disputant nescio quas impias novitates; et nos conantur arguere, quod aliquid novum dicamus"; *ibid.*, 20: ". . . ne nos insuper appellent haereticos. . . ."

67. Aug., *De gest. Pel.* 25.

68. Aug., *Serm.* 294.1: "et quia iam prolixus erat, et de illo terminando cogitabatur, non tanta dicta sunt de tanta quaestione, quanta in tanto periculo a sollicitis dici debuerunt."

69. Aug., *Serm.* 294.20: "Ut amici exhortamur, non ut inimici litigamus."

70. *Ibid.,* 19, v. Cyprian, *Ep.* 59.

71. Aug., *Serm.* 294.2–14.

72. Aug., *De pecc. mer.* 1.23.

73. Pel., *Dem.* 9; *Virg.* 4.

74. Aug., *Serm.* 294.16–18.

75. Aug., *Serm.* 294.16: ". . . dicunt et parvulos turbant, 'Si de peccatore peccatores nati sunt, quare non de baptizato iam fideli, cui remissa sunt universa peccata, iusti nascuntur?' . . . vis ut de baptizato baptizatus nascatur, cum videas de circumciso non nasci circumcisum?" Cf. *De pecc. mer.* 3.16 f.

76. *Ibid.,* 18: "Unde credunt? quomodo credunt? fide parentum. si fide parentum purgantur, peccato parentum polluti sunt." Cf. *De pecc. mer.* 3.2.

77. *Ibid.,* 20: ". . . eos talia disputantes nos appellare possimus forsitan, si velimus, nec tamen appellamus."

78. *Ibid.*

79. Aug., *De gest. Pel.,* "Postea coepit ad nos fama perferre, quod adversus dei gratiam disputaret . . . postea vero quam in Africam venit, me absente nostro, id est Hipponensi litore exceptus est, ubi omnino, sicut comperi a nostris, nihil ab illo huius modi auditum est, quia et citius, quam putabatur, inde profectus est."

80. Aug., *De gest. Pel.* 51: "Et ego quidem in epistola mea, quam protulit, non solum ab eius laudibus temperavi, sed etiam, quantum potui, sine ullius commotione quaestionis de dei gratia recti sapere admonui."

81. The date of Augustine's letter to Pelagius is not possible to fix with certainty. One must assume it to have been written before early 415, when Augustine received his copy of Pelagius' *De natura,* as it is not conceivable that he could have written such a polite note after reading that work. For a terminus *a quo* there is only the vague evidence of Augustine (*De gest. Pel.* 51) that the letter was written after he had already begun to receive rumors that Pelagius was opposing the grace of God. It would seem most natural to suppose that Pelagius, having left Africa in 411, would have written to Augustine sometime after arriving safely in the Holy Land. Augustine's reply would find a natural place sometime in or close to 412. The treatise in which Augustine gives evidence of having read Pelagius' commentary (*De pecc. mer.* 3.1) comes from 412.

82. Aug., *Ep.* 186.1: "Nam cum hoc de illo aliquamdiu fama iactaret, non utique facile credendum fuit—solet quippe fama mentiri—sed propius, ut crederemus, accessit, quod librum quendam eius ea prorsus persuadere molientem, quae gratiam dei per unum mediatorem dei et hominum hominem Christum Iesum generi humano impertitam

de fidelium cordibus creditam deleant, legimus traditum nobis a famulis Christi, qui eum talia docentem studiosissima audierant fuerantque sectati."

83. Aug., *Ep.* 186.1: "Nam et nos non solum dileximus, verum etiam diligimus eum; sed aliter nunc diligimus, aliter quando dileximus: tunc enim, quia nobis rectae fidei videbatur, nunc autem, ut ab his, quae inimica et adversa gratiae dei sentire dicitur, illius misericordia liberetur."

84. Aug., *De gest. Pel.* 46: "Postea coepit ad nos fama perferre, quod adversus dei gratiam disputaret. quod licet dolerem et ab eis mihi diceretur quibus crederem"; *ibid.*, 51: "iam enim audieram contra gratiam, qua iustificamur, quando hinc aliqua commemoratio fieret, aperta eum contentione conari."

85. Aug., *Ep.* 186.1: "Nam cum hoc de illo aliquamdiu fama iactaret, non utique facile credendum fuit—solet quippe fama mentiri."

86. Aug., *De pecc. mer.* 3.1: "Verum post paucissimos dies legi Pelagii quaedam scripta . . . quae in Pauli apostoli epistolas expositiones brevissimas continerent."

87. Aug., *Ep.* 186.2.

88. Aug., *De gest. Pel.* 47: "Cum vero mihi etiam liber ille datus esset a servis dei, bonis et honestis viris Timasio et Iacobo. . . . tum vero sine ulla dubitatione mihi claruit, quam esset christianae saluti venenum illius perversitatis inimicum."

89. Aug., *Ep.* 177.6. It is very likely also that the effect upon Augustine of Pelagius' *De natura* is closely related to the crescendo of serious opposition to Pelagius in the Holy Land. The agitation which Jerome had led among the Latin Christians there took on renewed vigor with the arrival on the scene in 415 of Orosius, whom Augustine had sent to see Jerome (Aug., *Ep.* 166.2). Orosius reports in Palestine that Augustine is at work on a writing against Pelagius' book *De natura* (Oros., *Lib. apol.* 3), which must mean that Pelagius' work had been received in Hippo before Orosius' departure. It is therefore most likely that Orosius knew well of Augustine's anxiety over this work. These circumstances support the thesis maintained in this chapter that Augustine's reading of *De natura* marks an important turning point. Orosius' hot-headed behavior in Palestine is what one might expect of a disciple who shared the animus but not the circumspection of Augustine. Cf. Loofs, *op. cit.*, p. 762. John Ferguson, *Pelagius* (Cambridge, 1956), pp. 82 f., has made the suggestion that the book which Orosius in Palestine reports Augustine as in process of writing might be the *De perfectione iustitiae hominis*. This is not possible. Orosius reports (*Lib. apol.* 3) that Augustine is writing *ipsius Pelagii*

prodentibus ac petentibus, which must refer to Timasius and James, onetime disciples of Pelagius (see Aug., *De nat. et grat.,* 1; *De gest. Pel.* 47; *Ep.* 179.2), to whom he addressed his work *De natura et gratia.* The *De perfectione iustitiae hominis* was written at the request of the bishops Eutropius and Paul and concerned the breviates of Celestius.

90. Aug., *De nat. et grat.* 10; cf. Pel., *Exp.* 46, 26–47, 13.

91. Aug., *De nat. et grat.* 10.

92. *Ibid.,* 21: "de eo disputandum est, quod per peccatum debilitata dicitur et immutata natura. . . . quomodo potuit humanam debilitare vel mutare naturam, quod substantia caret?" Cf. *Exp.* 44, 24 f.; 53, 11 ff.; 59, 2–16; 61, 17–21.

93. Aug., *De nat. et grat.* 21; cf. *Exp.* 44, 24; 61, 19–21.

94. Aug., *De nat. et grat.,* 23 f. Here Pelagius possibly has in mind a section in Augustine's *De libero arbitrio* (3.51 ff.) in which the author puts forward the view that the condition of punishment for man's original disobedience can itself be called sin; see especially 3.54 and 57.

95. Aug., *De nat. et grat.* 27–29.

96. *Ibid.,* 33 f.

97. *Ibid.,* 10: ". . . in Adam peccasse omnes non propter peccatum nascendi origine adtractum, sed propter imitationem dictum est." Cf. *Exp.* 45, 11; 45, 16–22; 47, 19; 48, 5 f.; 50, 6.

98. Aug., *Contr. duas epp. Pel.* 3.24; *De dono persev.* 4.

99. Aug., *Ep.* 190.22: "unde omnino apertissimi haeretici iudicantur, animas parvulorum nihil mali ex Adam trahere, quod sit lavacro regenerationis expiandum?"

100. See above, n. 97.

101. The following points may be noted for comparison between the fragments from the *De natura* and the commentary on Paul: (1) sinlessness is possible, see *De nat. et grat.* 8, 49–51, 53–58, and 69; cf. *Exp.* 44, 12 ff.; 61, 20 f.; 128, 11 ff.; 378, 4 f.; 351, 8 f. (2) Pelagius turns James 3:8 into a question, *De nat. et grat.* 16; cf. the same method of exegesis for Rom. 9:16 (a text of importance for Augustine's position) in *Exp.* 76, 13 ff. (3) Certain holy men of the Old Testament were without sin, a proposition which involves the interpretation of Rom. 3:23, *De nat. et grat.* 42–45 and 48; cf. *Exp.* 43, 15; 45, 11–21. (4) Christians are no longer "in the flesh," *De nat. et grat.* 60; cf. *Exp.* 53, 14 f.; 337, 15–18. (5) Flesh-substance cannot be contrary to spirit, because everything God made is good, *De nat. et grat.* 63 and 66; *Exp.* 62, 17 f.; 336, 15–18. (6) Paul's question at Rom. 7:24 is spoken from the point of view of one who has not yet been baptized, *De nat. et grat.* 64; cf. *Exp.* 60, 11–13; cf. also 56, 12 ff. and 58, 12 f.

102. Aug., *De nat. et grat.* 53: "Nam cum dicitur . . . ipsum posse arbitrii humani omnino non esse, sed naturae, sed auctoris naturae, dei scilicet, ecqui fieri potest ut absque dei gratia intellegatur, quod ad deum proprie pertinere censetur?" *Ibid.*, 59: "Ipsa . . . non peccandi possibilitas non tam in arbitrii potestate quam in naturae necessitate est. quicquid in naturae necessitate positum est, ad naturae pertinere non dubitatur auctorem, utique deum. quomodo ergo . . . absque dei gratia dici existimatur, quod ad deum proprie pertinere monstratur?"

103. *Ibid.*, 53–58.

104. See, e.g., *De correptione et gratia*, 29–32.

105. Aug., *De nat. et grat.* 62: "Non tunc de illa gratia quaestio est, qua est homo conditus, sed de ista, qua fit salvus per Iesum Christum dominum nostrum. . . . gratia ergo dei, non qua instituatur, sed qua restituatur, quaeratur; quae ab isto sola clamatur non esse necessaria, cum tacetur."

106. Pel., *Exp.* 32, 23 f.; 39, 12 ff.; 48, 22 f.; 353, 6 f.; cf. 246, 6.

107. Aug., *Ep.* 177.4; *De gest. Pel.* 61; *De grat. Chr.* 2.

108. Aug., *De nat. et grat.* 71–80.

109. Torgny Bohlin, *op. cit.*, pp. 46–103, with reff. to the previous philological studies of A. J. Smith.

110. See reff. given by Bohlin, pp. 46–56.

111. Aug., *Retract.* 1.8.6: "Ecce tam longe, antequam Pelagiana heresia extitisset, sic disputavimus, velut iam contra illos disputaremus," cf. *De nat. et grat.* 81.

112. The *De libero arbitrio* is commonly understood to have been written between the years 388 and 395 (*Retract.* 1.8.1); the two works, *Expositio quarundam propositionum ex epistula ad Romanos* and *Epistulae ad Romanos inchoata expositio* come from the year 394.

113. Aug., *De lib. arb.* 3.51–64. On the question of the guilt to be attached to this "sin," see chaps. 57 ("quae neque his neque Creatori tanquam culpanda tribuatur"), 63, and 64.

114. Aug., *De nat. et grat.* 54: "Voluntatis enim arbitrio ac deliberatione privatur, quidquid naturali necessitate constringitur."

115. *Exp.* 10, 9; 145, 7; 267, 15 and 17; 370, 15. *Dem.* 3 (18A–B).

116. Aug., *De nat. et grat.* 54.

117. Aug., *De lib. arb.* 3.2. Cf. the same distinction between necessity and will in Lactantius, *Div. instit.* 4.25 (quoted by Pelagius in Aug., *De nat. et grat.* 71), and Ambrose, *Comm. in Luc.* 6.77.

118. Aug., *De lib. arb.* 2.50: "Virtutes igitur quibus recte vivitur, magna bona sunt; species autem quorumlibet corporum, sine quibus recte vivi potest, minima bona sunt; potentiae vero animi sine quibus recte vivi non potest, media bona sunt"; 2.52: "voluntas ergo quae medium bonum est. . . ."

119. *Ibid.*, 50: "Virtutibus nemo male utitur; caeteris autem bonis, id est, mediis et minimis, non solum bene, sed etiam male quisque uti potest. Et ideo virtute nemo male utitur, quia opus virtutis est bonus usus istorum, quibus etiam non bene uti possumus."

120. *Ibid.* 51–53.

121. E.g., *Dem.* 3 (18A), 8 (22D). *De lib. arb.* (Aug., *De grat. Chr.* 5 and 19).

122. *De pecc. mer.* 2.30: "Quapropter nisi obtineamus non solum voluntatis arbitrium quod huc atque illuc liberum flectitur atque in eis naturalibus bonis est, quibus et male uti malus potest, sed etiam voluntatem bonam, quae iam in eis bonis est, quorum esse usus non potest malus, nisi ex deo nobis esse non posse, nescio quemadmodum defendamus quod dictum est: 'quid enim habes quod non accepisti (1 Cor. 4:7)?' nam si nobis libera quaedam voluntas ex deo est, quae adhuc potest esse vel bona vel mala, bona vero voluntas ex nobis est, melius est id quod a nobis quam quod ab illo est. quod si absurdissime dicitur, oportet fateamur etiam bonam voluntatem nos divinitus adipisci. quamquam voluntas mirum si potest in medio quodam ita consistere, ut nec bona nec mala sit. aut enim iustitiam diligimus et bona est et, si magis diligimus, magis bona, si minus, minus bona est, aut si omnino non diligimus, non est bona. quis vero dubitet dicere voluntatem nullo modo iustitiam diligentem non modo esse malam, sed etiam pessimam voluntatem. si ergo voluntas aut bona est aut mala et utique malam non habemus ex deo, restat ut bonam voluntatem habeamus ex deo." It is clear that in the first sentence of this quoted passage, Augustine obliquely acknowledges the theory of will as a *medium bonum* and even appears to hold it, whereas by the last sentence he has abandoned it. That the basic issue here remains of importance in the controversy with Pelagius can be seen at Aug., *De grat. Chr.* 19. Pelagius writes that man's *possibilitas utriusque partis* is like a fruitful and fecund root which, according to man's choice, produces either a bloom of virtues or a bramblebush of vices. Augustine answers that the same root could not bring forth good and evil fruits and that Pelagius' image contradicts the Lord's words, "A good tree cannot bring forth evil fruit, neither can a corrupt tree bring forth good fruit" (Matt. 7:8). After writing *De pecc. mer.* Augustine seems for a moment to waver at *De spir. et litt.* 58, where he defines *liberum arbitrium* as a *media vis* which can incline either toward faith or unbelief. Even here, however, the *voluntas* which believes is received from God. The position which Augustine enunciates at *De pecc. mer.* was to remain his settled conviction; see *De civ. Dei* 12.9.

123. Aug., *De lib. arb.* 1.29: "Ex quo conficitur ut quisquis recte honesteque vult vivere, si id se velle prae fugacibus bonis velit, assequa-

tur tantam rem tanta facilitate, ut nihil aliud ei quam ipsum velle sit habere quod voluit."

124. *Ibid.*, 3.52: "Cum autem de libera voluntate recte faciendi loquimur, de illa scilicet in qua homo factus est loquimur."

Chapter 6: THE THEOLOGY OF PELAGIUS

1. The chief studies on this subject are the articles by A. J. Smith in *J.T.S.* 19, 20, and 30 (1917–30) and the theological analysis, based largely but not wholly upon Smith's articles, of Torgny Bohlin, *Die Theologie des Pelagius und ihre Genesis* (Uppsala, 1957), pp. 46–103. Chap. 4 in the present book is intended to be a contribution to the source analysis of Pelagius.

2. Torgny Bohlin, *op. cit.*; Gerald Bonner, *St. Augustine of Hippo* (Philadelphia, 1963), pp. 312–93.

3. Georges de Plinval, *Pélage, ses écrits, sa vie, et sa réforme* (Lausanne, 1943); John Ferguson, *Pelagius: A Historical and Theological Study* (Cambridge, 1956) [see his list, taken from Plinval, on pp. 186 f.]

4. Bohlin, *op. cit.*, without discussing the literary question, confines his attention to the commentary on Paul, the letter to Demetrias, and the fragments from *De natura* and *De libero arbitrio*.

5. Both Plinval and Ferguson may be mentioned here. I am indebted in varying degrees to Plinval, Ferguson, Bohlin, and Bonner, and have not thought it worthwhile at a number of places to supply my footnotes with polemical references to these authors. The articles by Paul Marti in *Schweizerische Theologische Umschau* ("Die AuslegungsGrundsätze des Pelagius" [32, 1962, pp. 71–80], "Pelagius und seine Zeit" [32, 1962, pp. 167–75], and "Zur Ethik des Pelagius" [33, 1963, pp. 129–34]), based upon the pseudo-Jerome commentary in PL 30, show no awareness even of Souter's text of Pelagius' commentary and are of very limited value.

6. The fragments of the *De fide trinitatis* which we possess were successfully attributed to Pelagius by P. C. Martini, "Quattuor Fragmenta Pelagio Restituenda," *Antonianum* 13 (1938), 293–332. There is no reason to suppose that the fourth fragment, which Martini entitled *Contra Apollinaristas* (text pp. 332–34), is from the same work. As Martini himself admits (p. 318, n. 6), this may be (I should say probably is) from another, unknown work of Pelagius, on Christology. Martini's fragments from the *De fide trinitatis* are reprinted in *P.L.* Sup. 1, 1544–57, where they are identical with Fragmenta 1, 4, and 5. The Pelagian authorship of Fragmentum 2 in the same Migne Supplement (see col. 1108, text in P.L. 39, 2198–2200) has not been established. References to Pelagius' work on the Trinity will hereafter be

designated by the title *Trin.*, followed by the appropriate Migne column nos.

7. In *P.L.* Sup. 1, 1548 f. (cf. 1108) and 1557–60. The Migne editors misleadingly include these fragments among those from the work which they entitle *De trinitate*, i.e., *De fide trinitatis.* The fragments do not really concern the Trinitarian problem, and I venture the hypothesis that they are from an unknown work of Pelagius on Christology. It is not unlikely that Pelagius would have written such a work, which would have formed a parallel to that on the Trinity.

8. See reff. given in Souter 2, 553.

9. See, e.g., reff. given in Souter 2, 553. Bohlin, *op. cit.*, pp. 12–45, has recently called attention forcefully to the anti-Manichaean direction of much of Pelagius' thought. This element in Pelagius' thought had previously been recognized by Plinval, *op. cit.* (e.g., pp. 158 and 217) but not developed so extensively. Cf. Bonner, *op. cit.*, p. 317.

10. *Dem.* 3 (18A): "utriusque partis possibilitatem homini inserendo, proprium eius fecit esse quod velit, ut boni ac mali capax naturaliter utrumque posset."

11. *Dem.* 2–4 and 8. *Exp.* 22, 20; 23, 16 f.; 46, 14.

12. *Dem.* 7; *De nat.* (Aug., *De nat. et grat.* 34 and 35). The Latin phrase is usually "necessitas naturae."

13. Aug., *De lib. arb.* 3.2. Note that Pelagius (Aug., *De nat. et grat.* 71) also quotes Lactantius (*Instit. div.* 4.25) as giving expression to the distinction between *voluntas* and *necessitas*. And as Bohlin points out (*op. cit.*, p. 58), Pelagius would have found the distinction also in Ambrosiaster.

14. *De lib. arb.* (frag. Souter 1, P.L. Sup. 1, 1540). Hereafter references to Souter's fragments of this work will be cited by the appropriate column no. in this supplementary volume to the Latin Migne.

15. *Dem.* 3 (17C): "nec ipsa naturae violentia astringitur ad immutabilis boni necessitatem."

16. *De nat.* (Aug., *De nat. et grat.* 53 and 59); cf. *De lib. arb.* (Aug., *De grat. Chr.* 5).

17. *De nat.* (Aug., *De nat. et grat.* 53): "Nam cum dicitur, ipsum posse arbitri humani non esse, sed auctoris naturae, dei scilicet; ecqui fieri potest ut absque dei gratia intelligatur, quod ad deum proprie pertinere censetur?" Also *De lib. arb.* (Aug., *De grat. Chr.* 5).

18. *De nat.* (Aug., *De nat. et grat.* 59): "Ipsa non peccandi possibilitas non tam in arbitri potestate, quam in naturae necessitate est. quidquid in naturae necessitate positum est, ad naturae pertinere non dubitatur auctorem, utique deum. quomodo ergo absque dei gratia dici existimatur, quod ad deum proprie pertinere monstratur?"

19. *Dem.* 3 (18A); *De nat.* (Aug., *De nat. et grat.* 53); *De lib. arb.* (Aug., *De grat. Chr.* 19, and *De pecc. orig.* 14).

20. Cf. the discussion of the divine and human *posse* in Bohlin, *op. cit.*, pp. 17–19, 33. Bohlin overlooks the difficulty posed by Pelagius' *two* arguments for calling the "possibilitas non peccandi" a gift of grace.

21. *De lib. arb.* (Aug., *De grat. Chr.* 5): "unde quod propter calumniam vestram saepe repetendum est, cum dicimus hominem posse esse sine peccato, et confessione possibilitatis acceptae laudamus deum, qui nobis hoc posse largitus est, nec est ibi ulla laudandi hominis occasio, ubi solius dei causa tractatur."

22. *Exp.* 37, 14 f.; 178, 6 f.; 261, 10; 332, 20–333, 1; 346, 18 f.; 476, 7. *De lib. arb.* (Aug., *De pecc. orig.* 30). *De lege* 10 (116B).

23. Jerome, *Dial. adv. Pel.* 1.14; Jerome is here probably reflecting conversations with Pelagius or with members of Pelagius' circle. See also *Exp.* 180, 16; 246, 19–247, 10; 322, 1 f.; 519, 1–3.

24. *Exp.* 45, 11 f. and 16–22; 47, 17–19; 48, 5; 50, 5 f. *De nat.* (Aug., *De nat. et grat.* 10).

25. See above, chap. 5, pp. 73 and 82 f.

26. *De nat.* (Aug., *De nat. et grat.* 21): ". . . quaerendum puto quid sit peccatum: substantia aliqua, an omnino substantia carens nomen, quo non res, non existentia, non corpus aliquod, sed perperam facti actus exprimitur." Cf. *Exp.* 44, 24; 61, 19–21.

27. *De nat.* (Aug., *De nat. et grat.* 8, 10, 13, 34, and 54).

28. *De nat.* (Aug., *De nat. et grat.* 33, 34, 53, 54, 57).

29. *De nat.* (Aug., *De nat. et grat.* 21). *De lib. arb.* (frag. Souter, I, 1540, and 3, 1543).

30. *Exp.* 47, 7–9. Pelagius is here reacting against a doctrine of transmitted sin which he found in Ambrosiaster. See Bohlin, *op. cit.*, pp. 60 ff.

31. *De lib. arb.* (Aug., *De pecc. orig.* 14), cf. *De nat.* (Aug., *De nat. et grat.* 63).

32. *Dem.* 5 f.; *Vita* 7; *De nat.* (Aug., *De nat. et grat.* 42–44).

33. *Exp.* 45, 16–23; *Dem.* 5 (19D); *Vita* 7.

34. *Exp.* 46, 10–14; *Dem.* 8 (23A–B).

35. *Dem.* 6 (22A), on Job: "O virum ante evangelium evangelicum, et apostolicum ante apostolica praecepta. discipulum apostolorum, qui aperiens occultas divitias naturae, et in medium proferens, ex se quid omnes possimus, ostendit. docuitque quantus sit ille thesaurus animae, quem nos sine usu possidemus; et quod proferre nolumus, nec habere nos credimus."

36. *Dem.* 5 (20A and B).

37. *Dem.* 8 (23B); *De lib. arb.* (Aug., *De pecc. orig.* 30).

38. *Dem.* 8 (23B); *De lib. arb.* (Aug., *De pecc. orig.* 30).

39. *Exp.* 165, 2-7; 178, 6 f.; 324, 4 f.; 355, 2-4; 528, 10-12.

40. *Exp.* 325, 1-5.

41. *Exp.* 26, 16-27, 1.

42. *Exp.* 248, 14 f.

43. *Exp.* 355, 5.

44. *Dem.* 8 (23B); *De lib. arb.* (Aug., *De pecc. orig.* 30); *De nat.* (Aug., *De nat. et grat.* 42); *Exp.* 82, 8 ff. *Lib. eclog.* (Aug., *De gest. Pel.* 13).

45. *Exp.* 27, 22 f.; 48, 22; 57, 14 f.; 319, 19; 322, 10; cf. *Dem.* 16 (30D-31A).

46. *Exp.* 57, 18-22; 246, 19, etc.

47. *Exp.* 59, 6; 59, 12 f.; 90, 21; 164, 2 f.; 319, 4; 336, 3-6; *Dem.* 8 (23C), 17 (31D), 24 (38B); *De lib. arb.* (Aug. *De grat. Chr.* 43 and *De pecc. orig.* 30); etc.

48. *Dem.* 8 (23C); *Cel.* 10.

49. *De lib. arb.* (Aug., *De grat. Chr.* 43): ". . . qui nimia vitiorum consuetudine velut quadam teneretur necessitate peccandi, et quamvis bonum appeteret voluntate, usu tamen praecipitaretur in malum."

50. *Exp.* 59, 13: ". . . quam tamen necessitatem mihi ipse paravi."

51. *Dem.* 8 (23B–C), 17 (31D); *Exp.* 32, 8.

52. *Exp.* 205, 10 ff.; *Dem.* 23 (37C); *Cel.* 15.

53. *Exp.* 164, 2 f.

54. *De lib. arb.* (Aug., *De pecc. orig.* 30); *Exp.* 58, 21-59, 6; 319, 4.

55. *Exp.* 32, 7; 39, 9-14; 56, 15 ff.; 57, 8; 58, 2 f.

56. *Dem.* 17 (31D).

57. *Dem.* 8 (23C): "et miramur cur nobis per otium atque desidias nescientibus, etiam quasi ab alio sanctitas conferatur, qui nullam consuetudinem boni facimus, cum malum tamdiu didicerimus."

58. *Exp.* 56, 12 ff.

59. *Cel.* 10; *Dem.* 8 (23C–D), cf. *ibid.* 2 (16C–D).

60. *Exp.* 33, 5 f.; 39, 9-12; 114, 2 ff.; 320, 12 ff.

61. Cf. the ambiguous passage *Dem.* 3 (18C), where Pelagius praises the virtues of pagan philosophers whom he has himself seen. He does not in fact say that they are "without sin" but does aver that they demonstrate "quales a deo facti sunt." But then he immediately goes on to contrast the moral achievements of these virtuous pagans with the possibilities open to Christians, "quorum in melius per Christum natura et vita instructa est, et qui divinae quoque gratiae iuvantur auxilio." The passage is therefore, from a systematic point of view, confused and is to be seen chiefly as providing exhortatory material for the young Demetrias' reading. The praising of virtuous pagans is not characteristic of the writings of Pelagius; this passage is exceptional.

62. *Exp.* 60, 15 f. Also *ibid.* 335, 19.

63. *Exp.* 59, 17–60, 5.

64. *De lib. arb.*, frag. Souter 1 (1539–41) and 3 (1542 f.).

65. Pelagius can waver a bit as to whether in fact *all* men are lost in sin. He writes, for example (*Exp.* 45, 13): ". . . cum paene aput nullum iustitia remansisset, per Christum est revocata."

66. *Dem.* 6 (22A): "qui aperiens occultas divitias naturae, et in medium proferens, ex se quid omnes possimus, ostendit; docuitque quantus sit ille thesaurus animae, quem nos sine usu possidemus; et quod proferre nolumus, nec habere nos credimus."

67. *Exp.* 59, 5 f.; 336, 6.

68. *De nat.* (Aug., *De nat. et grat.* 8, 57, 59); *De lib. arb.* (Aug., *De grat. Chr.* 5, cf. 33); *Lib. fid.* 13. Cf. *Exp.* 61, 20 f., where the relation between the possibility of being without sin and the doctrine of creation is made clear. The proposition in the *Lib. eclog.* (Aug., *De gest. Pel.* 16), "posse hominem, si velit, esse sine peccato," Pelagius explains quite adequately as applying to men after conversion (*ibid.*): ". . . sed quoniam a peccatis conversus, proprio labore et dei gratia possit esse sine peccato."

69. *De nat.* (Aug., *De nat. et grat.* 8): "nam si idcirco tales fuerint, quia aliud esse non potuerunt, culpa carent."

70. *Ibid.*, 10.

71. *Ibid.*, 21.

72. *De lib. arb.*, frag. Souter 1 (1539–41) and 3 (1542 f.).

73. *De nat.* (Aug., *De nat. et grat.* 29).

74. *Ibid.*, 24.

75. *De lib. arb.* (Aug., *De pecc. orig.* 14).

76. *De lib. arb.* (Aug., *De grat. Chr.* 5). See the whole passage, particularly the latter section beginning with these words: "unde, quod propter calumniam vestram saepe repetendum est, cum dicimus hominem posse esse sine peccato, et confessione possibilitatis acceptae laudamus deum, qui nobis hoc posse largitus est . . . ." Cf. *De nat.* (Aug., *De nat. et grat.* 53), where the same considerations are evident.

77. Pelagius' work *De libero arbitrio* had the form, at least in part, of a dialogue with Jerome, as Souter's fragments make clear (*P.L.* Sup. I, 1539–43). That Jerome understood Pelagius' doctrine of the "possibilitas non peccandi" as indicated in the text is apparent at many places, e.g. *Ep.* 133.6.

78. *De lib. arb.* (Aug., *De grat. Chr.* 30): "ut quod per liberum homines facere iubentur arbitrium facilius possint implere per gratiam."

79. *De lib. arb.* (Aug., *De grat. Chr.* 43; *De pecc. orig.* 30); frag. Souter 1, 1540.

80. *De nat.* (Aug., *De nat. et grat.* 8, 49, 53, 57, 59, etc.); *De lib. arb.* (Aug., *De grat. Chr.* 5, 19, etc.); *Exp.* 61, 21.

81. *Exp.* 260, 8.

82. *Exp.* 253, 15 ff.

83. *Exp.* 320, 12: "Christus ergo, cui non erat iudicium mortis nec causa subeundae crucis et maledicti, pro nobis maledictum subiit, quia omnes rei mortis eramus et debiti ligno quasi maledicti, qui permansimus in omnibus quae scripta erant in lege." See also *ibid.*, 33, 2–13; 43, 12–14; 44, 6-11; cf. *Trin.* (1544–48, 1554–57); *Cont. Apoll.* (1557–60).

84. *Exp.* 33, 5 f.; 39, 9–12; 114, 2 ff.; 320, 12 ff.

85. *Exp.* 43, 13; 44, 6–11.

86. *Exp.* 52, 20; 420, 6; *Vita* 14 (1044); etc.

87. *Exp.* 3, 2; *Cel.* 3 f.; etc.

88. *Exp.* 245, 2; *De lege* 10 (116B); etc.

89. *Exp.* 339, 5.

90. *Exp.* 179, 2 f.

91. *Exp.* 3, 1: ". . . evangelia, quae supplementum legis sunt et in quibus nobis exempla et praecepta vivendi plenissime digesta sunt . . . ."

92. *Exp.* 244, 16–245, 5.

93. *De lib. arb.* (Aug., *De pecc. orig.* 30).

94. *Exp.* 246, 19–247, 10.

95. *Exp.* 61, 1 and 17–21; 62, 2; 63, 10 f.

96. *Exp.* 252, 4 f.; 398, 9–399, 5.

97. *Exp.* 466, 14 f.

98. *Exp.* 136, 5 f.

99. *Exp.* 136, 6 f.

100. *Exp.* 261, 12.

101. *Exp.* 31, 11 f.

102. *Exp.* 62, 2

103. *Exp.* 420, 6: "dimittendo peccata et doctrina sua et exemplo ab ira nos iudicii liberavit . . . ." See also *ibid.*, 509, 1–5.

104. *Exp.* 33, 10 f.

105. *Exp.* 44, 25.

106. *Cel.* 21.

107. *Exp.* 278, 12 ff.; 376, 6; 520, 15 f.; *Dem.* 27 (42A); *Vita* 7 (1037); *De lege* 3; *Lib. eclog.* (Jer., *Dial. adv. Pel.* 1.25 and 29).

108. *Exp.* 9, 15; 47, 18–20 and 25 f.; 69, 11; 246, 6; 346, 14; 352, 15; 454, 5. *De lege* 2 (106D and 107B).

109. *Exp.* 34, 20; 36, 15; 41, 15; 81, 13; 261, 22; 323, 3; 353, 10 f.; etc. See the reff. assembled in Souter 1, p. 70. Plinval is certainly wrong in suggesting ("Points de vues récents sur la théologie de Pé-

lage," RSR 46, 1958, p. 229) that Pelagius' words on justification by faith alone cannot be taken seriously as representing his real view but are to be attributed to the necessity imposed by Pauline exegesis. If this were the case, the words *sola fides* would not appear so repeatedly as they do in Pelagius, nor would Pelagius have added the non-Pauline word *sola* to his formulation. He clearly distinguishes the righteousness of faith from the righteousness of works, both of which he wants to uphold; see *Exp.* 81, 19–82, 1.

110. *Exp.* 346, 6–9.

111. *Exp.* 52, 6 f.; 226, 9; 437, 10; 453, 1–7; 509, 1–5.

112. J. B. Mozley, *A Treatise on the Augustinian Doctrine of Predestination,* 2nd ed. (London, 1878), p. 50 (cited in Bonner, *op. cit.,* p. 364); Bohlin, *op. cit.,* pp. 32–35. Bonner associates the enabling power of grace with baptism and does not see that Pelagius' language concerning baptism refers to a *status* of man before God as righteous and free of sin.

113. Aug., *De gest. Pel.* 30: ". . . gratiam dei et adiutorium non ad singulos actus dari sed in libero arbitrio esse vel in lege ac doctrina."

114. *De lib. arb.* (Aug., *De grat. Chr.* 29): "cum autem tam forte, tam firmum ad non peccandum liberum in nobis habeamus arbitrium, quod generaliter naturae humanae creator inseruit, rursus pro inaestimabile eius benignitate, quotidiano ipsius munimur auxilio."

115. See my article, "Pelagius' Veracity at the Synod of Diospolis," *Studies in Medieval Culture,* ed. John R. Sommerfeldt (Kalamazoo, 1964), pp. 21–30.

116. *De lib. arb.* (Aug., *De grat. Chr.* 8): "quam nos non, et tu putas, in lege tantummodo, sed et in dei esse adiutorio confitemur. adiuvat enim nos deus per doctrinam et revelationem suam, dum cordis nostri oculos aperit; dum nobis, ne praesentibus occupemur, futura demonstrat; dum diaboli pandit insidias; dum nos multiformi et ineffabili dono gratiae coelestis illuminat."

117. *Ibid.,* 11: "et quomodo stabit illud apostoli, 'deus est enim qui operatur in vobis et velle et perficere? [Phil. 2:13]' operatur in nobis velle quod bonum est, velle sanctum est, dum nos terrenis cupiditatibus deditos, et mutorum more animalium tantummodo praesentia diligentes futurae gloriae magnitudine et praemiorum pollicitatione succendit; dum revelatione sapientiae in desiderium dei stupentem suscitat voluntatem, dum nobis (quod tu alibi negare non metuis) suadet omne quod bonum est."

118. *Exp.* 400, 5–9; 453, 1–7; 509, 1–5.

119. *Exp.* 52, 6: "gratia vincendi et doctrinam praebuit et exemplum."

120. Cf. *Dem.* 2 (17C) and 10 (26A); *Cel.* 10; cf. Deut. 30:19 and Matt. 7:13 f.

121. *Exp.* 43, 10 f.; 67, 13–16; 139, 4; 248, 13.

122. *Exp.* 453, 1 (on Col. 1:10): "exposuit (i.e., Paulus) et posuit qua re semper obscure dicebat: hoc est, quo modo deus det velle et adiuvet atque confirmet, docendo scilicet sapientiam et intellectus gratiam tribuendo, non libertatem arbitrii auferendo, sicut in praesenti orat ut impleantur agnitione voluntatis eius in omni sapientia et intellectu spiritali, quo possint digne deo per omnia ambulare."

123. Plinval, *Pélage, ses écrits, sa vie et sa réforme* (Lausanne, 1943), p. 238 (quoted by Bohlin, *op. cit.*, p. 32).

124. *Exp.* 46, 3; 196, 14 f.; 202, 3–6; 275, 3 f.; 281, 5–284, 10; 376, 4 f.; 390, 4 f.; 408, 10–15; etc.

125. *Exp.* 104, 14 (on Rom. 13:11).

126. *Exp.* 388, 19–389, 2.

127. *Dem.* 9 (24A–B); *De lege* 3 and 4 (108D).

128. *Vita* 7.

129. *De lege* 3 (107D): "nam sine divinae legis et disciplinae coelestis scientia, difficile esse quemquam posse salvari, non meus sed divinus sermo probabit."

130. *Dem.* 9 (24B): "initium obedientiae est quid praecipiatur velle cognoscere."

131. *Cel.* 13 (340, 3–8); 14 (341, 4–8).

132. Aug., *De gest. Pel.* 2: ". . . non posse esse sine peccato, nisi qui legis scientiam habuerit."

133. The following should be compared: *Exp.* 32, 23 f.; 34, 19; 36, 14; 47, 25 f.; 69, 10 f.; 353, 10–13; 359, 15 f.; 454, 4 f.

134. See n. 109 above. Cf. the statement of Fr. Loofs, PRE 15 (1904), p. 753: "Das 'sola fide' hat vor Luther keinen so energischen Vertreter gehabt als Pelagius."

135. *Exp.* 319, 21: "perfecta fides est non solum christum, sed etiam christo credere"; *De lege* 2 (107B): "credens autem ille est iuxta scripturas qui ex toto corde crediderit . . . ."

136. *Exp.* 501, 15.

137. *Exp.* 81, 19: "talis est qui christo credit ille qui universam legem implevit" (text as in V); see also the lines following.

138. *Exp.* 377, 16: "aqua lavit corpus, animam doctrina mundavit, sicut ait at Hebraeos: 'aspersi corda a conscientia mala, et abluti corpus aqua munda'; ita et vos corpora uxorum continentia, animas mundate doctrinis."

139. *Dem.* 12; *Virg.* 9. Cf. *Exp.* 484, 6; 492, 5; 493, 8; 530, 18.

140. *De lege* 1 (106A): "manifestum est obedientiam ex animi consilio, non ex corporis materia procedere."

141. *De lege* 1 (105D–106B) and 2 (entire).

142. *De lege* 2 (107C): "... verbum, quo gloriatur anima ...."

143. *De lege* 2 (107C): "iam non videbitur ex corde, ut debuit, sed ex corpore credidisse, quod nequaquam fieri posse ratione ulla conceditur ...."

144. *De lege* 1 (105D): "ad plenum ergo te scire cupio, quod ex parte nosse te credo, ob hoc dominum et Dei verbum descendisse de coelis, ut assumpto naturae nostrae homine, humanum genus, quod ab Adam iacebat, erigeretur in Christo."

145. *Exp.* 68, 19: "secundum quod proposuit sola fide salvare quos praescierat credituros, quos gratis vocavit ad salutem"; 69, 7: "quos praesciit credituros, hos vocavit"; 74, 13: "aput deum fidei sunt merito separati"; this appears to be the view taken by Ferguson, *op. cit.*, p. 138, although he does not distinguish the issues clearly.

146. *Dem.* 28 and 30; *Virg.* 4; *Cel.* 15; *De lege* 9.

147. *Exp.* 60, 22: "praedestinare idem est quod praescire."

148. *Exp.* 68, 23–69, 1; 345, 20 ff.

149. See reff. in Souter, 1, p. 179.

150. *Exp.* 69, 9: "hoc autem ideo dicit propter fidei inimicos, ne fortuitam dei gratiam iudicarent."

151. *Exp.* 69, 7–12; 74, 9–16; 75, 3 ff. and 20 ff.; 85, 10 f.; 345, 20 ff.

152. *Exp.* 68, 23–69, 1 (reading with MS V): "praedestinavit ut qui conformis fuisset in vita esset conformis in gloria."

153. *Ep. ad Innoc.* (Aug., *De grat. Chr.* 34): "illi ideo iudicandi atque damnandi sunt, quia cum habeant liberum arbitrium, per quod ad fidem venire possent et dei gratiam promereri, male utuntur libertate concessa"; *De lege* 2 (107B): "sed gratia quidem gratis peccata dimittit, sed cum consensu et voluntate credentis. ... credens autem ille est iuxta scripturas qui ex toto corde crediderit. et si ex tota cordis arce credendum est, ut ex credulitatis merito baptismum fidei detur, acqua non sufficit baptizato, quae credentis animum in corde non attingit." Cf. *Exp.* 74, 5 and 13.

154. Cf. Aug., *De gest. Pel.* 30, 32, and 40, where Augustine complains of Pelagius' inconsistency in this regard at the Synod of Diospolis.

155. See *De lege* 2 and cf. Pelagius' whole exegesis of Rom. 7, *Exp.* 54–60.

156. *De lege* 2 (107B): "sed gratia quidem gratis peccata dimittit, sed cum consensu et voluntate credentis."

157. Aug., *De pecc. orig.* 16: "aut quia dicit ideo infantes non in eo statu esse in quo fuit Adam ante praevaricationem, 'quia isti prae-

ceptum capere nondum possunt; ille autem potuit, nondumque utuntur rationalis voluntatis arbitrio, quo ille nisi uteretur, non ei praeceptum daretur.' "

158. *Lib. fid.* 7: "baptisma unum tenemus, quod iisdem sacramenti verbis in infantibus quibus etiam in maioribus, asserimus esse celebrandum."

159. The remission of sins relative to infant baptism was an issue among at least some Pelagians from an early date, as is apparent from its appearance in the first of Augustine's anti-Pelagian works, *De pecc. mer.* 1.22 f.

160. Aug., *De pecc. orig.* 21: " 'quis ille tam impius est, qui cuiuslibet aetatis parvulo interdicat communem humani generis redemptionem?' "

161. *Exp.* 34, 19 (on Rom. 3:28): "et hic de eo dicit, qui ad Christum veniens sola fide salvatur"; 36, 14: "convertentem impium per solam fidem iustificat, non per opera quae non habuit"; see the reff. collected above in n. 133.

162. *Exp.* 32, 4 ff.; 34, 9–19; 81, 21 ff.; 82, 20–24; *Vita* 13. Cf. *Dem.* 9 (24C); *Virg.* 6; *Cel.* 5 and 14. A lingering perfectionist doctrine of the Church appears in Pelagius, formed around a strictly moralistic interpretation of Eph. 5:27, and stated in such a way that Christians who incur the stain of guilt thereby separate themselves from the Church but may always be restored by *paenitentia*. See, *inter alia, Exp.* 128, 11 ff.; 378, 1–6 (*n.b.* MS V); *Virg.* 11 (241, 8 ff.); *Dem.* 24 (38C–D); *De lege* 1 (106B); *Vita* 9; *Lib. fid.* 7.

163. *Virg.* 4 (228 f.); *Cel.* 15; *Exp.* 378, 2 ff.; *Dem.* 25 (40, 13).

164. *Exp.* 37, 1: "ob hoc fides prima ad iustitiam reputatur, ut de praeterito absolvatur et de praesenti iustificetur et ad futura fidei opera praeparetur."

165. *Exp.* 12, 3–12; 44, 8 ff.; 172, 16–22; 364, 13 ff. *Trin.* (1554–57), etc.

Index